Nilh Izá Sptákwlhkalh
·················
niɬ ʔizá sptákʷɬkaɬ
·················
These Are Our Legends

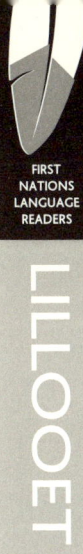

FIRST NATIONS LANGUAGE READERS

LILLOOET

Nilh Izá Sptákwlhkalh

niɬ ʔizá sptákʷɬkaɬ

These Are Our Legends

Narrated by Lillooet Elders

Transcribed and Translated by Jan van Eijk

Illustrated by Marie Abraham

FIRST NATIONS UNIVERSITY OF CANADA

University of Regina Press

Copyright © 2015 Jan van Eijk and Lilwat7ul Culture Centre*

*Note: All royalties from the sale of this book will go to the Lilwat7ul Culture Centre (formerly the Mount Currie Cultural Centre). The stories recounted herein remain the intellectual property of their creators.

All rights reserved. No part of this work covered by the copyrights hereon may be reproduced or used in any form or by any means—graphic, electronic, or mechanical—without the prior written permission of the publisher. Any request for photocopying, recording, taping or placement in information storage and retrieval systems of any sort shall be directed in writing to Access Copyright.

Printed and bound in Canada at Marquis. The text of this book is printed on 100% post-consumer recycled paper with earth-friendly vegetable-based inks.

Cover and text design: Duncan Campbell, University of Regina Press

The artwork in this volume is by Marie Abraham, a Lillooet artist from Mount Currie, British Columbia.

Library and Archives Canada Cataloguing in Publication

Nilh izá sptákwlhkalh—These are our legends / narrated by Lillooet elders ; transcribed and translated by Jan van Eijk ; illustrated by Marie Abraham.

(First Nations language readers : Lillooet) Title also appears in Lillooet syllabics. Issued in print and electronic formats. Text in Lillooet with English translation.

ISBN 978-0-88977-396-7 (paperback).—ISBN 978-0-88977-397-4 (pdf)

1. Lillooet language—Readers. 2. Lillooet language—Glossaries, vocabularies, etc. 3. Lillooet Indians—Folklore. 4. Indians of North America—British Columbia—Folklore. I. Eijk, Jan van, 1950-, translator, transcriber II. Title: These are our legends. III. Nilh izá sptákwlhkalh. IV. Nilh izá sptákwlhkalh. English. V. Series: First Nations language readers

PM2261.N54 2015   497'.943   C2015-905387-0

10 9 8 7 6 5 4 3 2 1

University of Regina Press, University of Regina
Regina, Saskatchewan, Canada, S4S 0A2
tel: (306) 585-4758 fax: (306) 585-4699
web: www.uofrpress.ca

U OF R PRESS

We acknowledge the financial support of the Government of Canada. / Nous reconnaissons l'appui financier du gouvernement du Canada. We acknowledge the support of the Canada Council for the Arts for our publishing program. This publication was made possible through Creative Saskatchewan's Creative Industries Production Grant Program.

CONTENTS

Foreword—vii

Húýlhkan ptakwlh—ix

On the Language of the Lillooet—xvii

niɬ ʔizá sptákʷɬkaɬ—1

Nilh Izá Sptákwlhkalh / These Are Our Legends—23

1. I á7eṅwasa nḱyap
   The Two Coyotes—25

2. Weq̓w ti nḱyápa
   Coyote Drowns—29

3. Ta nḱyápa múta7 ta tśúquṁa
   Coyote and Chickadee—33

4. Ti nḱyápa múta7 ti skalúl7a
   Coyote and Owl—37

5. Ti stalhálama múta7 i stsmáĺt.sa i míxalha
   Grizzly Bear and Black Bear's Children—43

6. Ta sṁéṁlhatsa múta7 ta skalúl7a
   The Girl and the Owl—49

7. Ta sqáycwa uĺlusmíntali ta míxalha
   The Man who Stayed with the Bear—61

Lillooet-English Glossary—71

Foreword

I am very happy to be able to include this volume in our First Nations Language Readers series. When this series was first conceived, for the publisher then known as the Canadian Plains Research Center, the scope of the series was to be restricted to the northern Great Plains. With the evolution to the University of Regina Press, this series was able to take on new life and new directions. Still, with previous volumes in Saulteaux (Ojibwe), Blackfoot, and western dialects of Cree, the old boundaries had not yet been crossed, nor had we yet had the opportunity to present texts outside of the Algonquian family of languages. With this volume of ancient stories from the Lillooet (Salish) people of interior British Columbia, our new declared promise and scope is made manifest.

I am even happier to be able to include this volume in our series for another reason. I have had the privilege of working with my friend Jan van Eijk for over twenty years at SIFC/First Nations University. I know of his dedication to the Lillooet people: the Elders with whom he has worked and the youth for whom we work to ensure a future that includes their language. I am especially pleased to play some small part in helping him to present this collection of Lillooet legends in a new format, perhaps for a larger audience, but still first and foremost for the Lillooet people.

As we do step beyond the Plains in our quest to make this a truly national collection of texts, I hope the larger audience continues to find the value inherent in these volumes and calls for more: more stories from your own communities, more stories from the story keepers and the story makers, more stories from those allies who have worked and continue to work with the Elders to record and preserve their wisdom and the knowledge that must be passed down to the younger generations. This is a call to be answered with many voices.

Arok Wolvengrey
sqapts, 2015

Húýlhkan ptakwlh

"I am about to tell a *sptakwlh*." This is the way in which Martina LaRochelle opens her story "The Girl and the Owl" that is included in this collection, and it is indeed the traditional opening line of a Lillooet Elder when starting a *sptakwlh*, a word that has been translated as 'legend' or 'myth', but that is better translated as 'ancient story forever'. Typically, *sptakwlh* relate events that happened long ago, when the world was young, humans and animals interacted frequently and could take each other's shape, and when powerful beings (often referred to as "Transformers," "Culture Heroes" or "Tricksters") roamed the earth, performing deeds that were powerful and impressive, testifying to their courage, cunning and compassion, or on the other hand engaging in actions that were foolish or otherwise reprehensible (and getting their just deserts), thereby teaching us important moral lessons about proper behaviour and its rewards or about improper behaviour and its consequences. As such, these ancient stories contain lessons that are relevant forever, as our translation of *sptakwlh* indicates.

A major character in Lillooet *sptakwlh* is Coyote, a Trickster whose character spans the entire gamut of human qualities, from very good to very bad. For example, in this collection's first story, we see the intelligence of Coyote revealed in his sly word play with the other Coyote (making this first story also a great illustration of Lillooet verbal humour). The following two stories, however, go on to show Coyote becoming the victim of his own foolishness, laziness, and carelessness. In many ways, Coyote makes us look into a mirror where we can see both our desirable and our less desirable character traits.

Aside from being exciting and entertaining, and containing moral lessons, these stories also often explain how animals, plants or the landscape acquired their present shape (as in "The Girl and the Owl," where we learn how the great horned owl got his big eyes and the lines under his eyes). Thus, *sptakwlh* function on many levels and they deserve our abiding respect, reflected in the fact that in olden days they could only be told during wintertime and after sundown and were subject to other protocols, such as the fact that the storyteller could not be interrupted, except by a hearty *i ay!*, roughly translatable as 'come on, tell us more!', and indicating that the audience definitely had not fallen asleep yet.

(There is also another line of Lillooet storytelling, called *sqwéqwel*, which deal with more recent events and are not subject to the restrictions that *sptakwlh* were subject to. The publication of a selection of *sptakwlh* here, and in Van Eijk and Williams (1981), where they first appeared, is not meant to disrespect the ancient protocols, but to allow as wide an audience as is possible to share in the wisdom of these stories.)

The entertaining part of *sptakwlh* often derives from their delicious and subtle sense of humour, and examples of this abound in the collection presented here, whether that be the gullibility of one of the protagonists in Bill Edwards' "The Two Coyotes," who easily falls for a verbal trap set by his fellow coyote, or Coyote's greed and laziness (both duly punished) in Rosie Joseph's "Coyote Drowns." Typically, the fun and sense of humour are here blended with moral lessons, underscoring the holistic nature of traditional First Nations teachings. We see that same blending in Bill Edwards' "Coyote and Chickadee," where Coyote's mocking questioning of Chickadee's hunting skills and marksmanship are quickly punished by one well-aimed arrow fired by Chickadee (something Coyote could have avoided had he not been so scatterbrained as to go mouse-hunting when his life is in acute danger), and where, having been revived by his comrade, he thinks he has just fallen asleep after he has laid dead for so long (an entire winter) that his hide has come off rotting! In Rosie Joseph's "Coyote and Owl," it is Coyote's dissatisfaction with his own talents and his desire for having Owl's night vision that leads him to be smartly outwitted by Owl. Grizzly Bear's behaviour in Adelina Williams' "Grizzly Bear and Black Bear's Children" can be best described as purely psychotic, and her punishment is appropriately gruesome (and hilarious at the same time in that mighty Grizzly is no match for a bunch of determined ants who resent Grizzly's invasion of their real estate and invade Grizzly in return!).

Martina LaRochelle's "The Girl and the Owl" and Bill Edwards' "The Man Who Stayed with the Bear" are more serious in that the girl in Martina's story learns to grow up and not draw unwarranted attention to herself, while the unsuccessful hunter in Bill's story faces the heartrending scene when, returning from yet another unsuccessful hunt, he overhears his wife telling their hungry children that their father will soon bring home lots of food. To protect his family from starvation, the man must acquire great hunting skills, and he does so, paradoxically, by sparing the life of a black bear—making this story also a fine illustration of the close relationship between the Lillooet and the other creatures with whom they share this earth.

However, both "The Girl and the Owl" and "The Man Who Stayed with the Bear" contain strong elements of humour as well, for example in the girl's disgust at the awful fare that Owl brings home for her to prepare as their shared meal, or the bear's deadpan, "Say, my friend, I am glad that you did not shoot me," when the man decides not to try his (hitherto very questionable) hunting luck on the bear. (A detail in Bill's story that is only accessible to speakers of Lillooet is the pun contained in the man's desperate cry *zuqwcenlhkán kelh t́u zúqwkan* 'I will go without food till I die' playing on *zuqw* 'to die' that occurs twice in this sentence.) In several ways, these last two stories, like the ones that precede them in the collection, demonstrate the profound literary qualities that are inherent in Lillooet oral literature, including the delightful language play and punning, that can only be captured imperfectly in translation.

Other details include the importance of the number "four" in Lillooet culture (and many other First Nations cultures), as evidenced by the four times that Coyote is jumped over by his comrade as part of the revival ritual performed by the latter in "Coyote and Chickadee," or the four arrows that are magically fixed by the bear in "The Man Who Stayed with the Bear." Also, the matter-of-fact references in this latter story to defecation and urination when the man is about to hibernate with the bear demonstrate the healthy attitude of First Nations culture towards bodily matters, avoiding both false shame and vulgarity, both of which are unfortunately too common in white oral culture.

I can think of no better summary of the above, and of no better introduction to these stories, than what my friend and colleague Lorna Williams wrote in the introduction to the 1981 collection where they were first published:

> The education of the young was the responsibility of all adults in the community. The practical day to day skills were taught through observation and practice: observation of adults performing the task, then practice by the young. The *sqwéqwel* was used mainly to pass along information that was of a more historical nature and to tell of personal life experiences. The third way was the use of the *sptakwlh*. These stories were told by the elders in the family, usually in the evening. The *sptakwlh* was the way in which the rules of conduct were taught.

Wenácw tu7!

Collecting the stories

The *sptakwlh* in this collection relate directly or indirectly to my field work on Lillooet, which was carried out between 1972 and 1984 (including my full-time employment at the Mount Currie Curriculum Centre, 1978–1984). The texts were collected (tape-recorded) by various persons in the years 1972–

1979, and transcribed and translated by me. The transcriptions and translations were then checked by me with the consultants from whom the stories were recorded. The *sptakwlh* told by Rosie Joseph were taped by Dr. Gordon Turner, while "Grizzly Bear and Black Bear's Children," told by Adelina Williams, was taped by Dr. Lorna Williams. The *sptakwlh* told by Bill Edwards were taped by the late Dr. Aert Kuipers. "The Girl and the Owl" was told by Martina LaRochelle and was taped by me, and I wish there was a way to capture on paper the magnificent way she told it, her voice a stirring sequence of perfectly timed cadenzas. There was also a slight hesitation before her opening line, for she had been told the story was pagan, which might explain her partial disclaimer at the end (*cw7aoz hem ti7 kwas wenácw, sptakwlh ti7* 'this is not true, it is a sptakwlh'). Yet, this concluding statement detracts nothing from the value of this story or the magnificent way she tells it.

During my stay in Mount Currie, when I could not consult Martina LaRochelle or Bill Edwards, who lived in Lillooet and Pavilion respectively, I checked or re-checked a number of these stories with the help of Mrs. Marie Leo of Mount Currie, who carried out her task with exemplary thoroughness and deep respect for the storytellers.

As is mentioned above, the stories included here were originally published in 1981, as *Cuystwí Malh Ucwalmícwts (Lillooet Legends and Stories)*. The few typos in that volume are quietly corrected here, and I have also made some minor changes to the original translations, to reflect my deepened understanding of the language. There are also a few words and small sentence fragments that are audible on tape, including a cassette tape of the stories in the 1981 edition that was compiled by the Mount Currie Cultural Centre (and will hopefully be converted to digital format soon), but that for some reason do not appear in the 1981 edition and have been restored here. As is to be expected in stories that are told off-the-cuff and not read from a written text, the tape also contains a few false starts, and repetitions or hesitations where the speaker temporarily has to collect her or his thoughts. (These minor slips are here edited to reflect the form intended by the speakers.) Also, due to the fact that the stories were not collected under ideal (i.e., studio) conditions, and the speakers' voices fall and rise according to the natural rhythm of the language, the reader of these texts should be alert to the fact that some words and minor fragments are difficult to hear on the tape. (There is a very brief fragment in "Coyote and Chickadee" that I still cannot understand and that is indicated with [..] in this volume.)

Also, on page 64 (second last paragraph), Bill Edwards says on the tape *Nilh túʔ stsúnas* 'and he told him', and on page 66 (first paragraph) he says *Nilh túʔ smaysnás iż* 'and he fixed them', the versions given here, but the 1981 edition has *Nilh túʔ stsúnem* 'and he told him' (literally, 'and then he was told'), and *nilh túʔ smayscítem* 'and he fixed them for him' (literally, 'and then they were fixed for him'), which, for complex grammatical reasons that fall outside this volume, I would expect and which probably result from my original editing of the text. Bill Edwards' phrases are restored here out of respect for this outstanding story teller.

Acknowledgements

This project would not have been possible without the profound knowledge and tireless assistance of the four Lillooet speakers who so kindly introduced me to the fascinating world of their rich cultural heritage. I am also deeply grateful for their patience during the checking sessions, in which they fielded my never-ending questions with great insight into the complexities and subtleties of their language, and with a delightful sense of humour. A special word of thanks is in order for Mrs. Marie Leo, whose conscientious treatment of these texts is credited above and gladly repeated here. The sadness I feel at the passing of these great teachers is tempered by the fond memories I have of them and the joy I feel every time I read these stories.

Gordon Turner, Lorna Williams, and Aert Kuipers also deserve my abiding gratitude for their extremely important contributions to this project. Marie Abraham's artistic talents deserve to be credited for the wonderful way in which they have added to the overall appearance of this volume.

Húýlhkan ptakwlh

My academic career would have ground to a complete halt had it not been for First Nations University of Canada (formerly Saskatchewan Indian Federated College), which hired me in 1989 and thus can take justified pride in helping to make this volume (and all my other linguistic contributions since 1989) possible. Above all, I wish to express my gratitude to Arok Wolvengrey for his groundbreaking work on, and ongoing oversight of, the First Nations Language Readers series that is being produced by the University of Regina Press. The present volume, and those that have already appeared in this series, would not have been possible without Arok's tireless dedication to this project (and his appropriately pitiless pursuit of me when I threatened to fall behind on my instalments to this volume—one could not wish for a better Slothhunter Pursuivant when attention to a project, once started, begins to slacken).

As always, I remain deeply grateful to my wife, Sonja, for her love, support and encouragement during times good and bad, and to my sons, Jesse and Mark, whose growth from little rascals into fine young men with very successful careers has added so much joy to my life.

On the Language of the Lillooet

Lillooet is an Interior Salish language spoken in an area about 160 to 300 kilometres north by northeast from Vancouver. The language falls into two closely related and largely mutually intelligible dialects: a northern one, spoken in an area containing the communities of Pavilion, Fountain, Bridge River, Lillooet, and Cayoose Creek, and a southern one, spoken in Mount Currie, Samahquam, Skookumchuck and Port Douglas. The central communities of Seton Lake and Anderson Lake (D'Arcy) probably represent a mix of both dialects, but that is an issue I have not been able to explore in any detail. Long-established patterns of mutual contacts and intermarriage between the two main dialect areas have led to a further blending of the various dialects. A map of the Lillooet-speaking area is provided in Van Eijk (1997) and Van Eijk (2013), and a slightly more detailed version in Davis and Van Eijk (2014).

The language went into steep decline in the twentieth century (mostly as a result of the disastrous residential school policy), but it has seen a revival in recent years, with active language classes and the ongoing output of a large number of curriculum materials in and about the language. (See www.USLCES.org for a catalogue of curriculum materials produced by the Upper St'át'imc Language, Culture and Education Society.)

Phonology

Lillooet vowels are given in Table 1 below, while consonants are given in Table 2 on the following page. Phonemes marked with subscript dot are retracted (i.e., retracted tongue-root with simultaneous tensing of the tongue muscles). Phonetic details are provided in Van Eijk (1997) and Van Eijk (2013). There are two borrowed phonemes, the vowel a̯u and the consonant ṭ, which occur only in a few words, and not in any of the texts included here.

	Front	Central	Back	
High	i		u	basic
High	i̯		u̯	retracted
Mid		ə		basic
Mid		ə̣		retracted
Low		a		basic
Low		ạ		retracted

Table 1. Lillooet Vowel Phonemes

Lillooet employs dynamic stress (marked with the acute), which is phonemic, as in **máqa?** 'snow' vs. **maqá?** 'Death Camas' ("poison onion"). Stress is also mobile, as in **cún-as** 'he (-as) tells (cun) him' > **cun-tumúɬ-as** 'he tells us (-tumuɬ).'

As for phonotactics, the language allows fairly complex consonant clusters, as in **?alkst** 'to work' (northern dialect), but not as complex as in, for example, Nuxalk (Bella Coola), for which see Nater (1979 and 1984).

On the Language of the Lillooet

Manner of Articulation			bilabial	dental	lateral	palatal	velar	labio-velar	uvular	labio-uvular	glottal
Obstruents	Stops	−vd	p	t			k	kʷ	q	qʷ	
		+glot	ṗ				k̇	k̇ʷ	q̇	q̇ʷ	ʔ
	Affricates	−vd				c ç					
		+glot		ċ	ƛ̇						
	Fricatives	−vd			ɬ	s ṣ	x	xʷ	x̌	x̌ʷ	h
		+glot									
Sonorants	Nasals	+vd	m	n							
		+glot	ṁ	ṅ							
	Laterals	+vd			l ḷ						
		+glot			l̇ ḷ̇						
	Glides	+vd	w	z		y	ɣ		ʕ	ʕʷ	
		+glot	ẇ	ż		ẏ	ɣ̇		ʕ̇	ʕ̇ʷ	

Table 2. Lillooet Consonant Phonemes

Lillooet morphophonemics are relatively simple and include: (a) deletion (indicated with square brackets, as in cúɬ-xit 'to point (cuɬ) s.t. out to (-xit) s.o.' > cúɬ-xi[t]-c-as 'he (-as) points it out to me (-c)'); (b) insertion of h between vowels, as in -ci 'you (object)' > -cih in cuɬ-xi[t]-cíh-as 'he points it out to you'; (c) the change of -s (homophonous marker for one of several transitivizing suffixes and the third person possessive) to -c after ɬ or s, as in kʷis 'to drop, get dropped' > kʷis-c 'to drop s.t.' (cf. qam̓t 'to get hit' > qam̓t-s 'to hit s.o., s.t.'), x̌iɬ 'to be done in a certain way' > x̌iɬ-c 'to do s.t. in a certain way, to treat s.o. in a certain way'; (d) phoneme harmony, in that a root with plain (non-retracted) phonemes will require non-retracted phonemes in a suffix, while retracted phonemes in a root require retracted phonemes in a suffix, as in ʔáma 'good' > ʔama-wílx 'to get better, to recover from an illness' vs. qə̣l 'bad' > qə̣l-wị́lx 'to get spoiled, break down'; (e) the change (non-optional in some cases, optional in others) of z ẓ to y ẏ before a coronal consonant, as in huẓ 'to be about to do s.t.' > húẏ-ɬkan (húẓ-ɬkan) 'I am about to do s.t.'; (f) the change of -kan 'I', -kaxʷ 'you (sing.)', -kaɬ 'we/our', -kalap 'you (pl.)' to -ɬkan, -ɬkaxʷ, -ɬkaɬ, -ɬkalap after resonants and vowels (non-optional) and (optional, though rare) after obstruents; (g) the change of -su 'your (sing.)' to -sw before vowels (and -cw after ɬ or s and before a vowel), as in páq̓ʷuɬ 'cache' > ta‿páq̓ʷuɬ-cw‿a 'your cache' (see the section on morphology below for the use of the underloop (‿)); and (h) glottalization of resonants as resulting from certain suffixes or from interior reduplication (for which see the section on morphology below), as in x̌zum 'big' > x̌zum̓-qʷ 'big animal' (-qʷ 'head; animal'), or twit 'good hunter' > twi<w̓>t 'boy' (i.e., 'little hunter', see the morphology section below for the angular brackets).

The status of schwa (a cover term for both ə and ə̣) is somewhat unstable, in that schwa may be deleted in some cases and inserted in others, as in pəq 'white' > pq-us 'bald eagle' (-us 'head, face'), but ʕʷuyt 'to sleep' > ʕʷúyt-əqʷ (n.ʕʷúyt-əqʷ) 'sleepy-head (dull, dumb)' (-qʷ 'head'). The vowel a alternates with h under the same circumstances as where əC alternates with C, as in ʔáma 'good' > ʔámh-us 'beautiful' (-us 'face). We see a similar pattern with aʔ and ʔ, as in pálaʔ 'one' > palʔ-úlm̓axʷ 'one area' (-ulm̓axʷ), but s.pzuʔ '(wild) animal' > s.pzú<za>ʔ 'bird' (the latter with interior [diminutive] reduplication, as detailed in the morphology section below). Remaining morphophonemic changes are minor and do not warrant a detailed discussion here.

In addition to the Amerindianist orthography that is in use for the language (as in the examples used so far in this introduction), there is also a practical orthography that was developed in the 1970s by Van Eijk with input from members of the Mount Currie community and that relies solely on the letters of the Latin alphabet. The correspondence between the two systems is as follows (Amerindianist/Practical): p/p, t/t, c/ts, c̣/t̲s̲, k/k, kʷ/kw, q/q, qʷ/qw; ṗ/p̓, c̣/t̓s̓, ƛ̓/t̓, k̓/k̓, k̓ʷ/k̓w, q̓/q̓, q̓ʷ/q̓w; s/s s̲/s̲, ɬ/lh, x/c, xʷ/cw, x̌/x, x̌ʷ/xw; m/m, m̓/m̓, n/n, n̓/n̓, l/l, l̓/l̓, l̲/l̲, l̲̓/l̲̓, y/r, y̓/r̓, ʕ/g, ʕ̓/g̓, ʕʷ/gw, ʕ̓ʷ/g̓w, w/w, w̓/w̓, y/y, y̓/y̓, z/z, z̓/z̓; h/h, ʔ/7; a/a, ạ/ao, i/i, ị/ii, u/u, ụ/o, ə/e, ə̣/v. Since the practical orthography writes c kʷ qʷ (Amerindianist) as ts kw qw, the combinations ts kw qw (Amerindianist) are written t.s k.w q.w in the practical orthography. The glottal stop is not written word-initially in the practical orthography (as in ʔác̓x̌ən/átsxen 'to see s.o., s.t.') but is written when a glottal stop-initial word or root receives a prefix (indicated with the period (.) in the Amerindianist transcription), as in s.ʔac̓x̌-s/s7atsxs 'to watch over s.o., s.t.' Instead of the superscript apostrophe to mark glottalization, both the practical orthography and the Amerindianist transcription also allow an apostrophe following the letter, as in p' instead of ṗ. Next to ao, ii, o, and v, the phonemes elsewhere represented as t̲s̲, s̲, l̲, l̲̓ are written ts, s, l, l̓.

The alphabetical order in the glossary (pp. 71–89), which lists the words in the practical orthography, is as follows: a, ao, c, cw, e, g, g̓, gw, g̓w, h, i, ii, k, k̓, kw, k̓w, l, l̓, l̲, l̲̓, lh, m, m̓, n, n̓, o, p, p̓, q, q̓, qw, q̓w, r, r̓, s, s̲, t, t̓, ts, t̓s̓, t̲s̲, u, v, w, w̓, x, xw, y, y̓, z, z̓, 7. Note that the glossary does not have examples of words starting in certain symbols (e.g., there are no words listed here that start in o or v).

Morphology

Lillooet words fall into full words and clitics. Full words are either invariable (i.e., not allowing bound morphology) or variable, allowing any of the following morphological operations:

xxi

prefixation, suffixation (far more common than prefixation), various types of reduplication, one infix, compounding, and apophony (unproductive, except in one form of reduplication).

Prefixation is indicated with a period following the prefix when presented as part of a word, but with a following hyphen when quoted in isolation, as in n.citxʷ 'my (n-) house (citxʷ)'.

Suffixation is indicated with a hyphen preceding the suffix, both in a suffixed form and when quoted in isolation, as in citxʷ-s 'his/her (-s) house'.

Interior reduplication, which signals the diminutive, repeats the consonant before the stressed vowel and places the copy after the stressed vowel, the copy written between angular brackets, as in √kʷis (√ = root) 'small' > kʷi<kʷ>s 'small', or naxʷít 'snake' > naxʷə<x̌ʷ>t 'worm' (with a change a > ə that accompanies diminutive reduplication in a number of cases). In a number of cases there is a vowel that follows the consonant copy as a morphophonemic by-product and is also written between the angular brackets, as in huʔ '(a bit) more' > hú<hu>ʔ 'a little bit more', s.pzuʔ '(wild) animal' > s.pzú<za>ʔ 'bird'.

Augmentive reduplication (labelled "total" reduplication in a number of my other works on Lillooet) repeats the first CVC of the root and signals the augmentive, mostly plural or collective in nouns, and a repeated or intensified action in verbs. The CVC augment (which is stressed in some forms and unstressed in others, according to rules described in Van Eijk (1997)) is indicated with a following colon (:), as in s.núk̓ʷaʔ 'friend, relative' > s.nək̓ʷ:núk̓ʷaʔ 'friends, relatives', s.qayxʷ 'man' > s.qáy:qyəxʷ (via underlying s.qáy:qəyxʷ, with deletion of ə before y and insertion after y) 'men', məc-xál 'to write' > məc:məc-xál 'to write a lot'.

Final reduplication repeats the consonant after the stressed vowel. It signals a telic process (i.e., a process going towards a certain goal), often with the notion that the process is not entirely controlled by the entity involved in it. It is indicated with the equal-sign (=) at the end of a morpheme, and with angular brackets plus the equal-sign inside a morpheme, as in √puɬ 'to get boiled' > púɬ=əɬ 'to boil, be boiling', λ̓qʷ-áẃ<=wə>s 'to get together' (cf. s.λ̓qʷ-aẃs '(to be) together').

Infixation (indicated with swing brackets, {..}) is limited to the inchoative (ingressive) marker ʔ, as in √nuqʷ 'warm (atmosphere)' > nu{ʔ}qʷ 'to warm up, to get warmer'.

Apophony, as said above, is rare, except when it accompanies certain forms with interior reduplication, as in naxʷít 'snake' > naxʷə́‹xʷ›t 'worm'. Outside those formations we have an example in ɣə́p-ən 'to stand s.t. up', s.ɣap 'tree', ɣi{ʔ}p 'to grow, grow up'.

Compounding consists of the linking of two roots, usually with a connecting element aɬ, and represented in writing with the plus-symbol (+), as in ləṗ+aɬ+k̓ʷúna? 'buried (ləp) salmon roe (k̓ʷúnaʔ)' or qəḷ+aɬ+tmíxʷ 'storm' (qəḷ 'bad,' tmixʷ 'land, earth, world, cosmos, weather').

Morphological operations may be combined in one form, as in √xiẇ 'raw' > xí{ʔ}‹xə›ẇ 'raw (but s.t. that should have been cooked)', or s.núk̓ʷaʔ 'friend, relative' > s.nək̓ʷ:núk̓ʷaʔ 'friends, relatives'. Multiple applications of the same type of reduplication are also possible, as in ka.mul:mul:múl˛a 'to stay in the water all the time' (√mul 'dipped in, put in water'), or twə́‹w›‹ẇə›t '(young) boy' (twi‹ẇ›t 'boy' < twit 'good hunter').

In transitive verbs, which combine object suffixes and subject suffixes, the former precede the latter, as in cun-tumúɬ-as 'he (-as) tells (cun) us (-tumuɬ)'.

Enclitics are indicated with a loop (˛) that follows proclitics and precedes enclitics, as in ta˛cítxʷ˛a 'the (ta˛) house' (with the 'reinforcing' element ˛a that is required by ta˛ and a number of other articles).

Syntax

Aside from a few adverbial or conjunctive markers, Lillooet is predicate-initial, as in ƛak ti˛n.k̓yáp˛a 'the coyote (n.k̓yap) goes (ƛak)', núk̓ʷʔ-an-c-as ti˛s.qáyxʷ˛a 'the man (s.qayxʷ) helps (núk̓ʷʔ-an) me'. Both the predicate and complement position can be taken by a form based on either a noun or a verb, as in n.k̓yap ti˛ƛák˛a 'the one who goes is a coyote', s.qayxʷ ti˛nuk̓ʷʔ-án-c-as˛a 'the one who helps me is a man'. The overlap between the categories 'noun' and 'verb' in this respect, and the feasibility of distinguishing them at all, is discussed in Kuipers (1968), Kinkade (1983), and Van Eijk and Hess (1986). In transitive constructions with both an object and a subject complement, the former generally precede the latter in the northern dialect, as in n.qix̌-c-áń-as ta‿s.k̓əm̓-c‿a ta‿s.k̓ʷú<k̓ʷ>m̓it‿a 'the child (s.k̓ʷú<k̓ʷ>m̓it) closed (n.q̓íx̌-c-ań) the door (s.k̓əm̓-c)', while in the southern dialect the subject complement generally precedes the object complement, as in pə́l-p-s-ás‿tu? ni‿n.s.kʷúz?‿a ni‿kapúh-s‿a 'my son (s.kʷúza?) lost (pə́l-p-s) his (-s) coat (kapúh)'. The dialect-based distinction between these constituent orders is not strict, as is shown by p̓am-an-ás‿tu? ta‿s.kix-əz?-íh‿a nə́ɬ‿qəx̌?-ič?-í‿a 'their (-ih) mother (s.kíx-za?) had thrown their dog skins (qəx̌?-íča?) into the fire' (p̓ám-an 'to throw s.t. into the fire'), which was recorded from Martina LaRochelle, a speaker of the northern dialect. For further details on this issue see Van Eijk (1995 and 2001).

Further comments on Lillooet syntax are given in the next section.

Concluding comments

A full analysis of the texts in this volume is not feasible because of space limitations, but a few aspects of the texts warrant a brief discussion. In the first place, the kataphoric pronoun niɬ often functions as a conjunction 'and then, and so' (in which case it usually combines with the discourse enclitic ‿ƛ̓u?). It then also requires a factualized construction (signalled with the nominalizer s-) in which the subject of an intransitive verb is marked with possessive affixes (as in níɬ‿ƛ̓u? s.wa?-s pu?yaxʷ-ám 'and then he (-s 'his') was hunting mice') and the subject of a transitive verb is marked with transitive subject suffixes (as in níɬ‿ƛ̓u?‿tu? s.ɬáp-n-as 'and then he forgot [what he was doing]'). (The examples in this paragraph, and the next, are all taken from "Coyote and Chickadee," included in this volume.)

In addition to the factual paradigm (limited to dependent clauses), Lillooet also employs an indicative paradigm (used in main clauses), as in ƛ̓ák‿kʷu? 'he was going', or ʔacx̌-n-ás‿kʷu? 'he saw him', and a subjunctive paradigm (used in both main and dependent clauses, and usually introduced with ɬ̩ in the latter, as in l.cʔá̩ka núkʷuṅ ɬʃʷúy̓t-an 'I must have slept here'). All three paradigms (which largely overlap in their transitive sub-paradigms) allow auxiliary constructions, which are fully stressed and usually based on **waʔ** 'to be (busy)' in the indicative paradigm, as in **wáʔ-ɬkan píx̌əm̓** 'I am hunting', but a proclitic construction in the other paradigms, as in **xʷʔa̩z lá.tiʔ kʷasu̩ zúqʷ-s kʷu̩s.tám̓** 'you won't kill anything with that' (**kʷasu̩** 'that you').

Natural Lillooet discourse and story telling are impossible without the use of a large number of discourse particles (either full words or enclitics), such as **ƛ̓uʔ**, a general discourse marker broadly translatable as 'well, but, so, for sure', etc., or reportative **kʷuʔ**, which indicates that one is relating something that one has not witnessed oneself but that one has been informed about by others. For that reason, **kʷuʔ** is prevalent in *sptakwlh*, as these refer to events that took place in a distant past.

Of the seven *sptakwlh* in this volume, four ("The Two Coyotes," "Coyote and Chickadee," "The Girl and the Owl," and "The Man Who Stayed with the Bear") are told by speakers of the northern (Fountain) dialect, while the other three ("Coyote Drowns," "Coyote and Owl," and "Grizzly Bear and Black Bear's Children") are told by speakers of the southern (Mount Currie) dialect. The only difference worth noticing here is that the northern dialect uses **ta̩** and **na̩** for respectively the 'present/known' and 'absent/known' articles, while the southern dialect has **ti̩** and **ni̩** instead. (The 1981 edition standardizes these articles to *ti* and *ni* for all four speakers, but **ta̩** *ta* and **na̩** *na* have been restored here in Bill Edwards' and Martina LaRochelle's texts.)

With regard to the Lillooet lexicon, there is also a somewhat melancholy meta-message in "The Girl and the Owl," in that Martina LaRochelle reflects on two words (*mek̓ilólya7*, approximately 'sticky matter', and *skig̓w*, approximately 'kept woman' or perhaps 'trophy wife') of which she admits that she does not know the precise meaning, but which were used in the version of the story told to her by her grandmother. Sadly, one almost sees old words fading away before one's eyes here, a fate that has befallen too many words in too many First Nations languages. The ongoing efforts, by both linguists and the Lillooet themselves, to preserve and revive the Lillooet language is therefore to be applauded even more.

Finally, the name "Lillooet" is derived from *Líłwat*, the ancestral name of the southernmost Lillooet-speaking bands (Teit 1906: 196). Instead of Lillooet, the term Státimcets (originally only referring to the language of the northernmost bands) is increasingly used in linguistic literature, and Ucwalmícwts (literally 'the language of the people' or 'the Indian language') in a number of curriculum materials.

References

Davis, Henry, and Jan van Eijk. 2014. "Lillooet Bird Names." *Anthropological Linguistics* 56: 78-99.

Kinkade, M. Dale. 1983. "Salish Evidence against the Universality of 'Noun' and 'Verb'." *Lingua* 60: 25-40.

Kuipers, Aert H. 1968. "The Categories Verb-Noun and Transitive-Intransitive in English and Squamish." *Lingua* 21: 610-626.

Nater, Henk F. 1979. "Bella Coola Phonology." *Lingua* 49: 169-187.

——. 1984. *The Bella Coola Language*. Ottawa: National Museum of Man Mercury Series. Canadian Ethnology Service Paper No. 92.

Teit, James A. 1906. *The Lillooet Indians*. The Jesup North Pacific Expedition, Vol. 2, Part V. Reprinted by AMS Press (New York), 1975.

van Eijk, Jan P. 1995. "POS and PSO in Lillooet." Paper submitted to the 30th International Conference on Salish and Neighbouring Languages.

——. 1997. *The Lillooet Language: Phonology, Morphology, Syntax*. Vancouver: UBC Press.

——. 2001. "POS and PSO in Lillooet, Part 2." Ms.

——. 2013. *Lillooet-English Dictionary*. Vancouver: University of British Columbia Occasional Papers in Linguistics, vol. 2.

van Eijk, Jan P., and Thom Hess. 1986. "Noun and Verb in Salish." *Lingua* 69: 319-331.

van Eijk, Jan (P.), and Lorna Williams (eds.). 1981. *Cuystwí Malh Ucwalmícwts (Lillooet Legends and Stories)*. Mount Currie, B.C.: The Ts'zil Publishing House.

niɫ ʔizá sptákʷɫkaɫ

(1) ʔi̓‿ʔá<ʔə>n̓was‿a n.k̓yap

ƛ̓ák‿kʷuʔ ká.tiʔ ʔi̓‿n.k̓yáp‿a, ʔá<ʔə>n̓was. nı́ɬ‿kʷuʔ‿ƛ̓u?
s.cut-s ta‿pə́<pə>lʔ‿a ɬlák‿ʔiz̓: "n.k̓yáp-ɬkan, tákəm‿ƛ̓u?
s.wat waʔ zəwat-ən-cál-it-as kʷənswa‿n.k̓yáp, k̓á‿maɬ
xʷʔaz̓ s.núwa kʷasu‿n.k̓yáp, pə<p>laʔ-ɬkáxʷ."

"xʷʔaz̓ ká.tiʔ, n.k̓yáp-kan‿ƛ̓uʔ ƛ̓it," cút‿kʷuʔ.

"xʷʔaz̓ ká.tiʔ, pə<p>laʔ-ɬkáxʷ. xʷúy‿maɬ zam̓, húy̓-
ɬkaxʷ zəwát-ən ɬkʷún-s‿a. húy̓-ɬkan ƛ̓aq̓ l.cʔá-wna
l‿ta‿n.ləṕ-xál-tn‿a, k̓alan̓-min̓-ɬkáxʷ‿ƛ̓uʔ ʔi̓‿ʔuxʷalmíxʷ‿a."

ƛ̓áq̓‿kʷuʔ ʔayɬ, ƛ̓áq̓‿kʷuʔ ʔá.tiʔ, ʔac̓x̌-n-ə́m‿kʷuʔ?
ʔə‿ki‿ʔuxʷalmíxʷ‿a. "tay, ƛ̓ak kən.tʔú ta‿n.k̓yáp‿a, nk̓yap
ká.tiʔ ta‿ƛ̓ák‿a." ƛ̓ák‿kʷuʔ, ka.xim̓‿a‿kʷú?‿tu?.

qʷacác‿kʷuʔ ʔayɬ ɬəl.kʷʔú niʔ na‿núkʷ‿a,
ka.ɬəx̌ʷ‿a‿kʷú?‿ƛ̓u?, qʷax̌t-min-it-ás‿kʷuʔ.

"ƛ̓ak mútaʔ ká.tiʔ ta‿pə́<pə>lʔ‿a, pə́<p>laʔ ká.tiʔ
ta‿ƛ̓ák‿a mútaʔ."

ƛ̓ák‿kʷuʔ, cíxʷ‿kʷuʔ ʔayɬ, pzán-as‿kʷuʔ na‿s.núk̓ʷaʔ-s‿a.

"ʔáʔhan-cu," cún-əm‿kʷuʔ, "ʔáʔhan-cu, qan̓im-ən-s-wít-
kaxʷ‿ha? n.k̓yáp-ɬkan, pə<p>laʔ-ɬkáxʷ s.núwa."

(2) wəq̓ʷ ti‿n.k̓yáp‿a

húy̓-ɬkan ʔayɬ ʔuxʷalmíxʷ-c-min̓ l.cʔá-wna ti‿n.k̓yáp‿a. s.təx̌ʷ‿tiʔ s.xə́<xə>m̓. ƛ̓ák‿kʷuʔ ká.taʔ, xáʔ-s‿a ʔə.tʔú-na ti‿qʷúʔ‿a. súx̌ʷast, ʔúqʷaʔ, ƛ̓ak mútaʔ x̌áƛ̓-əm.

wáʔ‿ƛ̓uʔ ʔá.tiʔ x̌íl-əm, níɬ‿ƛ̓uʔ s.kí{ʔ}<kə>i̓-s kʷas‿x̌áƛ̓-əm. níɬ‿ƛ̓uʔ mútaʔ s.ʔá.taʔ-s x̌aw̓:x̌aw̓:x̌áw̓n̓‿a ɬ‿ƛ̓ák-as ɬaʔ-s‿a‿ƛ̓úʔ‿a ti‿qʷúʔ‿a; ƛ̓ák‿kʷuʔ ká.tiʔ. plan mútaʔ ʔúqʷaʔ, plan mútaʔ.

cáma‿ƛ̓uʔ, níɬ‿ƛ̓uʔ s.xʷʔay-s kʷ‿s.xáƛ̓-ləx-s. ƛ̓ak ʔayɬ l‿ti‿qʷúʔ‿a. cúkʷ‿ƛ̓uʔ ʔi‿s.q̓ʷáx̌t-s‿a waʔ s.mul.

ƛ̓ák‿ƛ̓uʔ, lan mútaʔ ʔúqʷaʔ. cáma‿ƛ̓uʔ, níɬ‿ƛ̓uʔ s.láns‿ƛ̓uʔ mútaʔ waʔ ƛ̓ak qəm-p ti‿s.q̓ít‿a, níɬ‿ƛ̓uʔ mútaʔ s.kə́<k>{ʔa}w̓-s ʔá.taʔ ti‿s.ƛ̓ák-s‿a.

ʔá.tiʔ ʔayɬ ʕʷəlín-s‿a ɬwas‿ka.mul:mul:múl‿a l‿ti‿qʷúʔ‿a, ʕʷəlín-s‿a. plan mútaʔ ʔúqʷaʔ.

ƛ̓ák‿ƛ̓uʔ, níɬ‿ƛ̓uʔ s.əl.cʔá-s kʷƛ̓-ús-c‿a ɬ‿cíxʷ-almən-as ti‿qʷúʔ‿a. kʷí<kʷ>s‿ƛ̓uʔ ʔayɬ lá.tiʔ kʷas‿múi̓-c-am̓, lan ʔúqʷaʔ, ʔúqʷaʔ.

wáʔ‿ƛ̓úʔ ʔá.tiʔ x̌íl-əm ƛ̓u wəq̓ʷ‿tuʔ‿ƛ̓uʔ, niɬ‿k̓a‿túʔ‿ƛ̓uʔ s.zuqʷ-s.

(3) ta‿n.k̉yáp‿a múta? ta‿ćúqʷum̓‿a

n.k̉yáp‿ti? múta? c?á-wna kʷu‿s.ptákʷɬ. záx-t‿ti? sǝna?‿x̣u?, ɬq̓íq̓at‿x̣u? ta‿wa?‿zǝwát-n-an.

x̣ák‿kʷu? ká.ti? ta‿n.k̉yáp‿a, ?ać̌-n-ás‿kʷu? ta‿ćúqʷum̓‿a wa? ká.ti?. "wá?-ɬkaxʷ kán-ǝm?," cún-as‿kʷu? ta‿ćúqʷum̓‿a.

"?u, wá?-ɬkan píx̌ǝm̓."

?ać̌-xít-as‿kʷu? ta‿tǝ́x̌ʷ?ac-s‿a. "?u," cún-as‿kʷu?, "s.tam̓‿kɬ lá.ti? kʷa‿zúqʷ-s-axʷ l‿ta‿tǝ́x̌ʷ?ac-sw‿a? kʷi⟨kʷ⟩s-?úl, kʷi⟨kʷ⟩s-?úl! xʷ?a̲z lá.ti? kʷasu‿zúqʷ-s kʷu‿s.tám̓."

"xʷúy‿qa?‿zam̓, nas ?ǝ.t?ú-na x̌?íɬ‿a ?á.ti? l‿ta‿n.lǝṗ-xál-tn‿a, x̌ʷǝ́m‿x̣u? lá.ti? kʷ‿s.qam̓t-s-túmi-n ɬǝl.c?á."

"xʷuy," cút‿kʷu? ta‿n.k̉yáp‿a, níɬ‿kʷu? s.x̣ak-s ?á.ta?, cíxʷ‿kʷu? ?á.ta? x̌?íɬ‿a. níɬ‿x̣u?‿tu? s.ɬáp-n-as ɬwas‿kán-ǝm, níɬ‿x̣u? ká.ti? s.wa?-s pu?y̓axʷ-ám.

kʷil̓-qs-xít-ǝm‿kʷu? ?ayɬ ɬǝl‿t?ú ɬǝl‿ta‿ćúqʷum̓‿a, kɬ-aka?-xít-ǝm‿kʷu? ?á.ti?, pút‿x̣u? qám̓t-s-tum; q̓mín-n-ǝm‿kʷu? lá.ti?, niɬ s.zuqʷ-s.

níɬ‿kʷu? lá.ti?‿ti? s.kic-s, tákǝm ta‿sútik‿a, qapc. [..]

x̣ák‿kʷu? ká.ti? ta‿s.núk̉ʷa?-s‿a. "tay, s.tám̓-as‿k̉a núkʷun̓ kʷu‿s.záy-tǝn-su.

5

xʷʔáz̓ həm̓ ƛ̓uʔ kʷ‿s.xʷʔay-s kʷ‿s.záy-tən-ɬkaxʷ kʷasu‿wáʔ lá.tiʔ s.kic."

q̓əlx-anʔ-an-ə́m‿kʷuʔ, q̓əlx-anʔ-an-ə́m‿kʷuʔ, xʷʔúcin kʷ‿s.q̓əlx-ánʔ-an-əm.

txʷ-ús-əm‿kʷuʔ, ƛ̓ík̓-ləx‿kʷuʔ ʔayɬ. "ʔu, l.cʔá‿k̓a núkʷuṅ ɬʕʷúy̓t-an," cút‿kʷuʔ. plán‿kʷuʔ waʔ ka.ɬmə̣k‿a ʔi‿ƛ̓ámin-s‿a. "l.cʔá‿k̓a ɬʕʷúy̓t-an," cút‿kʷuʔ.

hú‹hu›ʔ mútaʔ sə́naʔ ɬəl.cʔá-wna, záx-t‿tiʔ cʔa kʷu‿s.ptákʷɬ‿ƛ̓uʔ. cúkʷ‿ƛ̓uʔ ta‿waʔ‿zəwát-n-an.

(4) ti‿n.k̓yáp‿a múta? ti‿s.kalú<l>ʔ‿a

wáʔ‿kʷuʔ l.cʔa ti‿n.k̓yáp‿a. waʔ xáƛ̓-miṅ-as kʷas‿ka.ʔáćx̌-m‿a ɬas‿sítst. plán‿kʷuʔ? ʔayɬ waʔ ʕáp-almən; waʔ ʔəm:ʔímn-əm ti‿s.kalú<l>ʔ‿a. níɬ‿ƛ̓uʔ s.cún-as: "tay, s.kalú<la>ʔ, kán-əm səs‿x̌zúm ʔi‿n.kʷƛ̓-ús-təṅ-sw‿a?"

níɬ‿ƛ̓uʔ s.cut-s ti‿s.kalú<l>ʔ‿a: "niɬ kʷənswa‿ka.ʔáćx̌-m‿a ɬas‿sítst," cút‿kʷuʔ. "ʔu," cút‿kʷuʔ ti‿n.k̓yáp‿a, "wáʔ-ɬkan ƛ̓it xáƛ̓-miṅ kʷənswa‿ka.ʔáćx̌-m‿a ɬas‿sítst, x̌íl-əm s.núwa. wáʔ-ɬkaxʷ kas-c, níɬ‿ƛ̓uʔ səs‿x̌zúm ʔi‿n.kʷƛ̓-ús-təṅ-sw‿a?"

7

"ʔu," cút‿kʷuʔ ti‿s.kalú<l>ʔ‿a, "ɬ‿x̌áx̌-miṅ-axʷ kʷas‿x̌zúm ʔi‿n.kʷx̌-ús-təṅ-sw‿a, níɬ‿x̌uʔ s.nás-cu kʷam kʷu‿qʷalíɬ. wáʔ-ɬkaxʷ‿x̌uʔ zəwát-ən ʔi‿qʷalíɬ‿a, kəla? q̇ix̌. məqʷ-ən-s-káxʷ, níɬ‿x̌uʔ s.qí<q>ċ-mín-axʷ. qí<q>ċ-mín-ɬkaxʷ lá.tiʔ x̌u plán‿x̌uʔ waʔ li<í>q kʷas‿ka.cə́s‿a. ʔalas-káxʷ‿x̌uʔ qí<q>ċ-min, níɬ‿x̌uʔ s.ʔáma-s, níɬ‿x̌uʔ s.ċəmq̇-án-axʷ, níɬ‿x̌uʔ s.ċəq̇-p-án-axʷ l‿ti‿n.kʷx̌-ús-təṅ-sw‿a ti‿núkʷ‿a, ċíla ti‿núkʷ‿a, níɬ‿x̌uʔ s.ċíla-s‿x̌uʔ ʔá.tiʔ. kəɬ-ən-ɬkáxʷ, plan‿kɬ x̌zum ʔi‿n.kʷx̌-ús-təṅ-sw‿a."

"xʷuy nas," cut, níɬ‿kʷuʔ‿x̌uʔ s.x̌ak-s ti‿n.k̇yáp‿a. x̌ak, kʷám‿kʷuʔ ʔi‿qʷalíɬ‿a, qí<q>ċ-əm‿kʷuʔ ʔayɬ lá.tiʔ x̌u plán‿x̌uʔ ʔayɬ waʔ li<í>q kʷas‿ka.cə́s‿a lá.tʔ ti‿s.qí<q>ċ-s‿a. ċəmq̇-án-as‿kʷuʔ ʔayɬ, níɬ‿x̌uʔ s.ɬúm-un-as l‿ti‿n.kʷx̌-ús-təṅ-s‿a, ċəq̇-p-án-as. wáʔ‿kʷuʔ ʔayɬ lá.tiʔ s.təq-s-ás x̌u ka.ʕʷuẏt‿á‿x̌uʔ.

My, s.təx̌ʷ‿x̌uʔ qə̣l ti‿s.x̌íl-əm-s‿a. kan-m-ás‿k̇a; xʷʔáy‿x̌uʔ kʷ‿s.zəwát-n-an ċílh-as n.kaʔ kʷ‿s.xiṅ-s kʷ‿s.ʕʷuẏt-s. xʷak, lan k̇ax ti‿s.qí<q>ċ-s‿a. níɬ‿x̌uʔ s.waʔ-s lá.tiʔ kəɬ-n-ás, cáma kəɬ-n-ás, xʷʔáy‿x̌uʔ kʷas‿ka.x̌íɬ‿a, plán‿x̌uʔ waʔ k̇ax.

qaṅim-ən-s-ás‿kʷuʔ? ʔayɬ ti‿s.kalú<l>ʔ‿a, lán-s‿a ʔayɬ múta? waʔ ʕáp-almən. "kalú<la>ʔ," cún-as, "kán-əm su‿x̌íɬ[-s]-tuṁx ʔə.cʔá? ʔáċx̌-ən, ċəq̇-p ʔayɬ ʔi‿qʷalíɬ‿a l‿ti‿n.kʷx̌-ús-tṅ‿a."

"ʔu," cút‿kʷuʔ ti‿s.kalú<l>ʔ‿a, "cuwaʔ-sú‿x̌uʔ s.záy-tən. kán-əm múta? saxʷ‿ʕʷúẏt?"

"xʷʔạ́z‿qaʔ səna? kʷənswa‿ʕʷúẏt, məs-kán‿x̌uʔ? ka.ʕʷuẏt‿á‿x̌uʔ."

"ʔáʔhan, cuwaʔ-sú‿x̌uʔ s.záy-tən!," cún-əm, "ɬ‿xʷʔạ́z-as‿ka kʷ‿s.ʕʷúẏt-su, lán‿ka‿tuʔ waʔ x̌zum ʔi‿n.kʷx̌-ús-təṅ-sw‿a. ʔáʔhan, ċila-wílx ʔayɬ múta? ʔi‿n.kʷx̌-ús-təṅ-sw‿a, wáʔ‿x̌uʔ qʷi<q>s."

cúkʷ‿tiʔ‿x̌uʔ.

(5) ti‿s.x̣ałálam‿a múta? ʔi‿s.cm-áɫt-s‿a ʔi‿míx̣ał‿a

waʔ kə́m̓-əm ʔi‿míx̣ał‿a, ti‿s.qac-əzʔ-íh‿a múta?
ti‿s.kix-əzʔ-íh‿a, nił səs‿húż. łwal-n-ít-as ʔi‿s.cm-aɫt-íh‿a
l‿ti‿s.ʔá⟨ʔ⟩c-əq-s‿a ti‿s.ɣáp‿a.

wáʔ‿kʷu? ká.ti? ti‿s.x̣ałálam‿a, pún-as
ʔi‿s.k̓ʷəm:k̓ʷú⟨k̓ʷ⟩m̓it‿a, nił‿x̣̓u? s.xəł-an-cút-s kʷas‿húż
ʔálk̓ʷ-ił.

waʔ ʔayɫ lá.ti? ʔálk̓ʷ-ił, x̣̓íq‿kʷu? ʔi‿míx̣ał‿a.

cút‿kʷu?: "wáʔ-łkan l.cʔa ʔalk̓-ən-tánih-an
wi‿s.cə⟨cə⟩w̓-qín̓-kst. ʔáma, ʔáma tsalapa‿wáʔ ká.kʷu?
Sə̓l-ílx, nas-kalá́p‿x̣̓u? múta?. ʔalk̓ʷ-ił-kán‿kł, kʷukʷ-xi[t]-
tumuł-kán‿kł."

qʷacac‿kʷu?‿ká‿tu? ʔi‿waʔ‿ʔə[s].s.cm-áɫt, nił‿x̣̓u?
s.lan-s kʷán-as, n.łam̓-án-as‿kʷu? ʔə‿ti‿n.cq-ús-tn‿a
ʔi‿ʔá⟨ʔə⟩n̓was‿a s.k̓ʷəm:k̓ʷú⟨k̓ʷ⟩m̓it, kʷúkʷ-un̓-as. x̣̓íq‿kʷu?
ʔi‿waʔ‿ʔəs.cúwaʔ, húż‿kʷu? cut: "plán-łkan q̓ʷəl-s lá.ti?
ʔi‿húż‿a s.ʔíłən-lap. wáʔ‿mał wáʔ-wi, wáʔ‿mał wáʔ-wi!"

nił‿kʷu?‿x̣̓u? lá.ti? s.ca{ʔ}xʷ-s ʔi‿míx̣ał‿a, t‿s.láns‿a waʔ? q̓ʷəl ʔi‿húż‿a s.ʔíłn-i, nił‿kʷu? s.cut-s: "waʔ-
łkan‿hə́m̓‿kł‿x̣̓u? l.cʔa, wáʔ‿mał wáʔ-wi!"

nił‿kʷu? ʔayɫ kəla[ʔ]-ʔúl n.łám̓-xal ti‿s.qác-əzʔ‿a
míx̣ał, waʔ? x̣íł-c-as ʔə.cʔá, nił-as‿kʷu? ti‿s.kʷə́⟨kʷ⟩zaʔ-s‿a
cə⟨cə⟩w̓-qín̓-kst.

"ʔu, kʷ‿s.wə́taʔ," cun-it-ás‿kʷu?, nił‿a‿xʷíł‿ka
ʔi‿s.cm-aɫt-káł‿a s.q̓ʷəl-xi[t]-túmuł-as." kʷan-it-ás‿kʷu? lá.ti?
ʔi‿waʔ‿s.k̓ʷíł s.kʷəz:kʷə́⟨kʷə⟩zʔ-i, nił‿kʷu?‿x̣̓u? s.qʷacác-i.

cʔás‿kʷu? ʔayɫ kál-im ti‿s.x̣ałálam‿a qəl:qəl-cín̓
kʷ‿s.xʷʔay-s kʷas‿łwál. ʔá.kʷu? cíxʷ-wit‿kʷu? ʔə‿ti‿s.ɣáp‿a,
nił‿x̣̓u? s.x̣̓kíw-lə x-i. wáʔ‿kʷu? lá.ti? s.qʷəm ʔi‿s.xʷú⟨xʷ⟩ż‿a
l‿ti‿s.ʔa⟨ʔ⟩c-əq-s‿á‿ti? ti‿s.ɣáp‿a.

xʷʔáz̲kʷuʔ ƛ̓u? ʔayɬ kʷ˰s.xiṅ-s, ƛ̓íq˰kʷuʔ ʔayɬ ti˰s.ƛ̓aɬálam˰a. "xʷúy˰maɬ xʷuy ɬlá.kʷuʔ, c̓áq̓-miṅ-i kʷ˰s.cə<cə>w̓-qíṅ-kst, ka.təq-s-kan˰á˰kɬ l.c?a x̌áẃṅ˰a."

"ʔu, ka.ƛ̓il˰a˰ƛ̓ú?˰a kaʔɬ, ka.ƛ̓íl˰a," cún-əm˰kʷuʔ, mícaʔq lá.tiʔ l˰ti˰s.qʷə́m˰a. lá.tiʔ ɬ˰ʔucz-ílx-axʷ, niɬ˰kɬ ʔá.taʔ s.c̓áq̓-miṅ-xí[t]-ci-m kʷ˰s.cə<cə>w̓-qíṅ-kst. ʔucz-ílx-kaxʷ, n.piʕ̓ʷ-q-ám̓-ɬkaxʷ."

xíl-əm‿kʷu? ʔayɬ cáẇcwa lá.ti?; mícaʔq‿kʷu?
I‿ti‿xʷu<xʷ>ż-áɬxʷ‿a. "xʷúy‿maɬ, lán-ɬkan ʔayɬ waʔ
s.ʔúcəz."

"ḱál-əm‿ƛ̓u? kaʔɬ, ʔucz-ílx‿ƛ̓u? kaʔɬ; xíɬ-c-kaxʷ ʔə.cʔá
ʔi‿s.kʷákst-sw‿a, n.piʕʷ-q-ám̓-ɬkaxʷ, níɬ‿kɬ‿ƛ̓u? s.xʷʔay-s
kʷ‿s.kəɬ-p-akaʔ-mín-axʷ kʷ‿s.cə<cə>ẇ-qín̓-kst."

xíl-əm‿kʷu? ʔayɬ ʔá.ti?, n.piʕʷ-q-ám̓‿kʷu?, xíɬ-c-as‿kʷu?
ʔə.cʔá ʔi‿s.kʷákst-s‿a.

wáʔ-s‿kʷu? lá.ti? qəl̓:qəl̓-cín̓ kʷ‿s.lan-s waʔ
s.kʷil̓, xʷʔáz‿kʷu?‿ƛ̓u? kʷas‿ċaq̓-min̓-xít-əm ɬlá.ti?
ʔi‿s.ḱʷəm:ḱʷə́<ḱʷ>m̓it‿a. cun-it-ás‿kʷu? kʷas‿ʕəl-ílx
kʷas‿ən.píʕʷ-q-am̓.

xʷʔáz‿kʷu?‿ƛ̓u? ʔayɬ kʷ‿s.xin̓-s, lán‿kʷu? ʔayɬ ʔuɬxʷ-
mín-əm ʔə‿ki‿s.xʷú<xʷ>ż‿a.

húż‿kʷu? ʔayɬ cut: "ʔananáh, ʔananáh, wáyt-kan
lá.kʷʔa, ʔananáh, wáyt-kan."

"ʔu, ka.ƛ̓il‿a‿ƛ̓úʔ‿a, ʔálas n.píʕʷ-q-am̓. cəq-w-ál-akaʔ
ʔə.cʔá-wna, ċaq̓-min̓-ə́m‿kɬ ʔá.taʔ kʷ‿scə<cə>ẇ-qín̓-kst."

wáʔ‿kʷu?‿ƛ̓u? ʔayɬ; "ʔananáh, ʔananáh."

zik-t‿kʷu?‿tú?‿ƛ̓u? ʔayɬ, lán-s‿kʷu?‿ḱa ʔayɬ n.ċaqʷ-q-án̓-
əm ʔə‿ki‿s.xʷú<xʷ>ż‿a.

cúkʷ‿ti?.

(6) ta͜s.mə́<m̓>ɬac͜a ͜múta? ta͜s.kalú<l>?͜a

húẏ-ɬkan ptakʷɬ, ptákʷɬ-min l.c?a ta͜s.mə́<m̓>ɬac͜a,
wa? ?ílal l.ta͜s.?ístkn͜a. wá?͜kʷu? lá.ti? ?ílal
ta͜s.mə́<m̓>ɬac͜a, xʷ?áy͜x̱u? kʷas͜ka.tə́kʷ͜a.

ní ɬ͜kʷu?͜x̱u? s.cut-s ta͜kʷə́<kʷa>?-s͜a: "xʷ?ə́z-as
kʷasu͜ka.tə́kʷ͜a, níɬ͜x̱u? n.s.huż šlít-ən ta͜s.kalú<l>?͜a,
c?as-min̓-cíh-as͜kɬ ta͜s.kalú<l>?͜a."

xʷ?áy͜x̱u? kʷas͜ka.tə́kʷ͜a, s.tam̓-as͜ḱá͜maɬ kʷa͜?ilal-
mín-as ta͜s.ḱʷú<ḱʷ>m̓it͜a, ta͜s.mə́<m̓>ɬac͜a. plán͜kʷu?͜ti?
wa? ?an̓w[as]-aszánuxʷ͜ḱa, kaɬ[as]-aszánuxʷ͜ḱa
ti?͜ta͜wa?͜?ílal.

xʷ?áy͜x̱u? kʷas͜ka.tə́kʷ͜a, níɬ͜kʷu?͜x̱u? s.cut-s
ta͜kʷə́<kʷa>?-s͜a: "?u, huż šlít-n-əm ta͜s.kalú<l>?͜a, huż
c?as-min̓-cíh-as."

xʷ?áy͜x̱u? kʷas͜ka.tə́kʷ͜a, níɬ͜kʷu?͜x̱u? ?ayɬ s.cut-s
ta͜kʷə́<kʷa>?-s͜a: "sima?-mín-͜maɬ l.c?a ta͜wa?͜?ílal,
xʷ?áy͜x̱u? kʷas͜ka.tə́kʷ͜a, sima?-mín͜maɬ, s.kalú<la>?."

xʷ?ə́z͜kʷu?͜x̱u? lá.ti? kʷ͜s.xin̓-s, put, c?ás͜kʷu?͜x̱ɬ
ta͜s.kalú<l>?͜a. "huhú hu, c?ás-min-ɬkan kʷ͜s.kíka?," cút͜kʷu?
ta͜s.kalú<l>?͜a.

"síma?͜x̱u?, síma?, sima?-mín͜x̱u?."

"huhú hu, c?ás-min-ɬkan kʷ͜s.kíka?," cút͜kʷu?
ta͜s.kalú<l>?͜a. xʷ?ə́z͜kʷu?͜x̱u? lá.ti? kʷ͜s.xin̓-s, x̱əp͜a͜kʷú?͜a
ta͜s.?ístkn͜a, niɬ͜a͜xʷíɬ͜ḱa ɬ͜?úɬxʷ-as ta͜s.kalú<l>?͜a
ta͜s.?ístkn͜a ɬəl.t?ú n.ɬá?-x-tn͜a ɬəl͜tsa͜?úɬxʷ-wit
?i͜?uxʷalmíxʷ͜a. ɬlá.ti? ɬ͜?úɬxʷ-as ta͜s.kalú<l>?͜a.
xʷ?ə́z͜kʷu?͜x̱u? ?ayɬ múta? kʷ͜s.xin̓-s, ka.x̱əḱ͜a͜kʷú?͜tu?
?ayɬ ta͜s.ḱʷú<ḱʷ>m̓it͜a, s.plán-s͜a͜xʷiɬ ?ayɬ kʷán-əm͜tu?
?ə͜ta͜s.kalú<l>?͜a.

n.ɬam̓-án-as͜kʷu? ?ayɬ lá.ti? l͜ta͜c̓lá?-s͜a, qʷul lá.ti?
?i͜našʷít͜a, ?i͜s.xʷú<xʷ>ż͜a, ?i͜takm͜á͜x̱u? lá.ti?,

ʔi̯ pəʕːpíʕ̓ɬh̯a, qʷúl̯kʷuʔ lá.tiʔ I̯ta̯c̓láʔ-s̯a, n.ɬam̓-q-án̓-as̯kʷuʔ ʔayɬ lá.tiʔ ta̯s.m̓ə́<m̓>ɬac̯a.

X̌uʔ s.niɬ-c ʔayɬ s.qʷacác-s, ʔúx̌ʷal̓-s-as kʷu̯cítxʷ-s̯k̓a tiʔ̯ta̯s.kalú<l>ʔ̯a. k̓a̯ɬwas̯ʔəs.cítxʷ, k̓a̯ɬ̯s.tám̓-as̯kən kʷas̯wáʔ ká.kʷuʔ, ta̯sáw̓t̯a.

wáʔ̯kʷuʔ ʔayɬ lá.tiʔ, níɬ̯X̌uʔ ʔayɬ səs̯əmʔám-min-as ta̯s.m̓ə́<m̓>ɬac̯a, m̓ʔam-min-ás̯kʷuʔ ʔayɬ lá.tiʔ. c̓ʔás̯kʷuʔ̯X̌ɬ ta̯s.m̓ə́<m̓>ɬac̯a, c̓ʔás̯kʷuʔ̯X̌ɬ, c̓íla qa{ʔə}ź-mín-as ta̯s.kalú<l>ʔ̯a ɬwas̯k̓ʷul̓-c-án̓-əm, X̌íq-xit-əm ʔi̯s.qʷyíc̯a, ʔi̯s.taʕ̓əsəzh̯a, ʔi̯s.m̓ú<m̓>tm̯̓a, ʔi̯takm̯á̯X̌uʔ. xʷʔaz̯ kʷas̯zəwát-n-as ɬwas̯kás ɬwas̯q̓ʷəl. xʷʔaz̯ múta? kʷ̯s.ka.c̓áqʷ-s-as̯a ɬwas̯x̌í{ʔ}<x̌ə>ẇ.

wáʔ̯kʷuʔ ʔayɬ, wáʔ̯kʷuʔ ká.tiʔ ta̯s.cicáʔ̯a.

"símaʔ̯qaʔ ʔə.c̓ʔá, símaʔ ʔə.c̓ʔá, húẏ-ɬkan ksn-án-cin," cún-as̯kʷuʔ ta̯s.cicáʔ̯a.

X̌uʔ s.niɬ-c ʔayɬ s.ksn-án-as, s.qʷál̓-n-as ʔayɬ ta̯s.cicáʔ̯a kʷu̯huẏ̯s.záy-tən-s ɬcíxʷ-as ʔá.kʷuʔ ʔúx̌ʷal̓ ʔə̯ki̯s.ʔístkn̯a, ʔə̯ki̯s.la:lí<l>təm̓-s̯a. níɬ̯X̌uʔ s.cún-as̯kʷuʔ ta̯s.cicáʔ̯a: "húẏ-ɬkaxʷ nas, kʷán-xi[t]-c kʷu̯xʷik̓-áź, kʷu̯zúc̓-mən, mək̓il̯-úlyaʔ," cút̯wiʔ. s.tam̓-as̯ká̯wiʔ múta? kʷɬ̯wáʔ mək̓il̯-úlyaʔ, xʷʔaz kʷənswa̯zəwát-ən, məs-kán̯X̌uʔ waʔ cut "mək̓il̯-úlyaʔ;" "mək̓il̯-úlyaʔ," cút̯kʷuʔ.

"ʔu," cút̯kʷuʔ̯X̌ɬ ta̯s.cicáʔ̯a, "ʔu," qʷacác̯kʷuʔ̯X̌ɬ ta̯s.cicáʔ̯a ʔá.kʷuʔ̯s.la:lí<l>təm̓-s̯a tiʔ̯ta̯s.m̓ə́<m̓>ɬac̯a. qʷacác̯kʷuʔ, níɬ̯kʷuʔ̯X̌uʔ s.X̌ak-s, X̌ak̯kʷuʔ ta̯s.cicáʔ̯a ʔá.tiʔ s.ʔístkn̯a, I̯ki̯waʔ̯ʔəs.cítxʷ.

"ʔah, ʔah," cút̯kʷuʔ̯X̌uʔ ta̯s.cicáʔ̯a, "c̓ʔas-min̓-xít-kan s.kíkaʔ ʔi̯mək̓il̯-úlyaʔ-s̯a, xʷik̓-áẏ-s̯a, zúc̓-mən-s̯a, ʔah, ʔah," cút̯kʷuʔ.

"ʔu saw̓t, símaʔ̯X̌uʔ, símaʔ̯X̌uʔ." qan̓ím̯ka̯wiʔ ká.tiʔ kʷɬ̯waʔ̯ʔəs.cítxʷ, qan̓ím. "símaʔ̯X̌uʔ, símaʔ̯X̌uʔ, saw̓t."

nít̓ k̓ʷuʔ ƛ̓uʔ múta? s.cút-s ƛ̓uʔ: "c̓ʔas-min̓-xít-kan s.kíkaʔ ʔi xʷik̓-áy̓-s a, məkil-úlyaʔ-s a, zúc̓-mən-s a." ʔu saẇt, ʔu saẇt.

"símaʔ ƛ̓uʔ." kʷán-as k̓ʷuʔ ʔayɬ ká.tiʔ ʔi xʷik̓-áz̓ a, məkil-úləyʔ a, ʔi..wəna?..zúc̓-mən-s a. "ʔu, qʷacác maɬ."

qʷacac-s-as k̓ʷúʔ ʔiz̓, cíxʷ-s-as k̓ʷuʔ ʔayɬ ʔá.k̓ʷuʔ ʔə ta s.kalúlʔ a, lá.k̓ʷuʔ l tsa wáʔ-s-as ta s.m̓ə<m̓>ɬac a. wáʔ k̓a wiʔ múta? zəwát-n-as k̓ʷu cítxʷ-s ta s.kalú<l>ʔ a.

wáʔ k̓ʷuʔ ʔayɬ lá.tiʔ ptínus-əm k̓ʷuʔ ta s.múɬac a ɬ húz̓-as kán-əm, nít̓ ƛ̓uʔ s.huy̓-s ɬlá.tiʔ q̓áy-ləx. məy-s-an-cút k̓ʷuʔ ʔayɬ, cíxʷ k̓ʷuʔ múta?, kʷán-as ʔi síkil a, tákm a ká.ti?. takəm k̓ʷúʔ ƛ̓uʔ k̓ʷ s.wín̓axʷ-s ʔi s.cíxʷ a k̓ʷ s.k̓ʷul-s ta s.m̓ə<m̓>ɬac a. húy̓ tiʔ lá.tiʔ máy-s-nas ta k̓ʷtámc-s a, nít̓ ƛ̓uʔ s.huy̓-s q̓áy-ləx ɬlá.tiʔ.

wáʔ k̓ʷuʔ, plán k̓ʷuʔ tú? tiʔ ʔayɬ qʷacác píx-əm̓ ta s.kalú<l>ʔ a, xʷíl-əm k̓ʷu s.q̓ʷəyíc múta? k̓ʷu tákəm ƛ̓uʔ ká.tiʔ wáʔ ƛ̓uʔ ƛ̓íq-s-as: ʔi s.m̓ú<m̓>tm̓ a, ʔi s.taʕəsəzh a, ƛ̓íq-xit-as ta s.kíʕʷ-s a, nít̓ tiʔ ʔayɬ waʔ nah-n-ás k̓ʷa s.kíʕʷ. s.tam̓-as k̓á maɬ tiʔ, xʷʔaz k̓ʷənswa zəwát-ən ɬ s.tám̓-as k̓ʷa s.kíʕʷ.

xʷʔaz múta? k̓ʷas x̌ək-xí[t]-c-as na n.k̓ʷə́<k̓ʷ>ʔ a ɬ s.tám̓-as k̓ʷa s.kíʕʷ. nít̓ k̓a wíʔ həm̓ ta s.əmʔam-min-ás a ta s.m̓ə<m̓>ɬac a.

wáʔ k̓ʷuʔ ʔayɬ lá.tiʔ ptínus-əm ta s.m̓ə<m̓>ɬac a ɬ húz̓-as kán-əm, nít̓ k̓ʷ s.ka.q̓áy-ləx-s a. cút k̓ʷuʔ: "ʔu, húy̓-ɬkan nas xʷíl-əm k̓ʷu síkil." kʷán-as k̓ʷuʔ ʔayɬ ʔi síkil a ká.tiʔ, ʔi qʷalíɬ a, ʔi takm á ƛ̓uʔ.

xʷuy, cʔás k̓ʷuʔ ƛ̓ɬ ta s.kalú<l>ʔ a, ƛ̓íq k̓ʷuʔ.

"símaʔ ƛ̓uʔ, ʔápaʔ, símaʔ ƛ̓uʔ." plan-s ʔayɬ waʔ məy-s-an-cút, huz̓ ʔúx̌ʷal. "n.ləq̓ʷ:laq̓ʷ-al-ús-əm maɬ," cún-as k̓ʷuʔ ʔayɬ ta s.kalú<l>ʔ a: "n.ləq̓ʷ:laq̓ʷ-al-ús-əm, x̌íl-əm-ɬkan ʔá.tiʔ, ʔác̓x̌-ən ɬk̓ún-s a ti ʔámh a n.s.k̓ʷƛ̓-us, məy-s-an-cút-kan."

xʷuʔ, n.ləq̓ʷ:laq̓ʷ-al-ús-əm‿kʷuʔ‿X̣ɬ lá.tiʔ ta‿s.kalú<l>ʔ‿a.
níɬ‿ḱa‿wiʔ zam̓ səs‿ən.cəʕ:cʕ-ál-us ta‿s.kalú<l>ʔ‿a.
n.ləq̓ʷ:laq̓ʷ-al-ús-əm‿kʷuʔ ʔayɬ lá.tiʔ, xʷuʔ, n.ṕukʷ-al-us-n-
ás‿kʷuʔ ʔayɬ ki‿síkil‿a, ki‿qʷalíɬ‿a, takəm‿kʷúʔ‿X̣uʔ
n.ṕukʷ-al-ús-n-as.

wáʔ‿kʷuʔ ʔayɬ lá.tiʔ ta‿s.kalú<l>ʔ‿a, xʷʔa̱z
kʷas‿ka.txʷ-ús-m‿a, níɬ‿X̣uʔ ʔayɬ s.q̓áy-lə-x-s ta‿s.m̓ə́<m̓>ɬac‿a,
q̓áy-ləx. xʷʔa̱z‿ḱa‿wiʔ put kʷ‿s.kə:káẃ-s kʷu‿tmíxʷ-s, wiʔ?
s.x̌ʷəm-s kʷ‿s.cixʷ-s ʔúx̌ʷal̓.

wáʔ‿kʷuʔ‿X̣uʔ lá.tiʔ, X̣íq‿kʷuʔ‿X̣ɬ ʔá.tiʔ ʔə‿ki‿s.la:l̓í<l̓>təm̓-
s‿a. My, cá{ʔ}xʷ‿kʷuʔ ʔayɬ ʔi‿s.la:l̓í<l̓>təm̓-s‿a.

wáʔ‿kʷuʔ ʔayɬ ká.tiʔ ta‿sáẃt‿a. níɬ‿kʷuʔ‿X̣uʔ s.cut-s:
"húy̓‿X̣uʔ X̣iq na‿s.kalú<l>ʔ‿a, húz̓‿həm̓‿X̣uʔ X̣íq-min̓-as cʔa
ta‿s.m̓ə́<m̓>ɬac‿a." cút‿kʷuʔ‿X̣ɬ ʔi‿núkʷ‿a ká.tiʔ: "tay, níɬ-
as lá.tiʔ ta‿sáẃt‿a kʷil̓-ín-al̓ap!"

xʷʔa̱z‿kʷuʔ‿X̣uʔ kʷ‿s.xin̓-s lá.tiʔ, cʔás‿kʷuʔ‿X̣ɬ
ta‿s.kalú<l>ʔ‿a, plan ʔayɬ waʔ n.x̌ʷəc:x̌ʷc-ál-us
ɬwas‿ḱa‿X̣uʔ‿kəns.kəɬ-n-ás ʔi‿síkil‿a mútaʔ ʔi‿qʷalíɬ‿a
l‿ta‿n.kʷX̣-ús-tən̓-s‿a ʔi‿takm‿á‿X̣uʔ n.ṕukʷ-al-ús-n-as
ta‿s.kalú<l>ʔ‿a. xʷʔa̱z‿kʷuʔ‿X̣uʔ kʷ‿s.xin̓-s, X̣íq‿kʷuʔ‿X̣ɬ
ta‿s.kalú<l>ʔ‿a. "huhú hu, cʔás-min̓-ɬkan na‿n.s.kíʕʷ‿a,"
cút‿kʷuʔ, "huhú hu, cʔás-min̓-ɬkan na‿n.s.kíʕʷ‿a."

xʷuʔ, cút‿kʷuʔ‿X̣ɬ ká.tiʔ ʔi‿təw:twə́<w><ẃə>t‿a ká.tiʔ
ʔi‿waʔ‿ʔəs.cítxʷ ká.tiʔ s.ʔístkn‿a: "nás-xit ʔá.kʷuʔ sáẃt‿tiʔ
ta‿s.m̓ə́<m̓>ɬac‿a, nás-xit ʔá.kʷuʔ."

xʷuʔ, cút‿kʷuʔ‿X̣ɬ ta‿s.kalú<l>ʔ‿a: "huhú hu, ʔúc‿tiʔ
ɬ‿níɬ-as na‿n.s.kíʕʷ‿a, huhú hu, ʔúc‿tiʔ ɬ‿níɬ-as
na‿n.s.kíʕʷ‿a," cút‿kʷuʔ‿X̣ɬ mútaʔ ta‿s.kalú<l>ʔ‿a.

"yək:yík-almixʷ ʔi‿s.ɣəp:ɣáp‿a," níɬ‿kʷuʔ‿X̣uʔ s.zək:zík-
t-s ʔi‿s.ɣáp‿a.

cút‿kʷuʔ‿X̣ɬ mútaʔ: "yək:yík-almixʷ ʔi‿ṕəq̓ʷ:ṕáq̓ʷuɬ‿a,"
níɬ‿kʷuʔ‿X̣uʔ s.zək:zík-t-s ʔi‿ṕáq̓ʷuɬ‿a ká.tiʔ.

cút‿kʷuʔ‿x̌ɬ: "yək:yík-almixʷ ʔi‿s.ʔəs:ʔístkn‿a,
níɬ‿kʷuʔ‿x̌uʔ ʔayɬ s.zəx̌q̇-s ʔi‿s.ʔəs:ʔístkn‿a.

níɬ‿kʷuʔ‿x̌uʔ s.cut-s ta‿pá<pə>lʔ‿a: "haḷa-xít-i‿maɬ
ta‿sáẇt‿a ta‿s.kíʕʷ-s‿a, haḷa-xít-i"—plan waʔ súxʷtn-as
kʷas‿ʔúc ɬwas‿s.kíʕʷ-s lá.tiʔ ta‿waʔ‿haḷa-xít-as—"haḷa-xít-i."

xʷuʔ, cút‿kʷuʔ ká.tiʔ ʔi‿təw:twí<ẇ>t‿a: "huż q̇əlzaʔ-s-
túm ta‿s.cutáɬ-kaɬ‿a." xʷuʔ, qʷacác‿kʷuʔ‿x̌ɬ ṗám-s-əm
ʔi‿s.qáy:qəyxʷ‿a lá.tiʔ n.q̇əlzaʔ-tn‿a, huż q̇əlzaʔ-s-twít-as
ta‿s.cutáɬ-ih‿a. plan lá.tiʔ waʔ ptínus-əm
ʔi‿təw:twə́<w><ẇə>t‿a t‿s.húẏ-s‿a k̇əz-akaʔ-mín-it-as
lá.tiʔ ta‿s.cutáɬ-ih‿a.

plan cukʷ kʷ‿s.ṗám-s-m-i. "xʷuy," cun-it-ás‿kʷuʔ ʔayɬ
ta‿s.cutáɬ-ih‿a, "húẏ-ɬkaɬ nas q̇əlzaʔ, kʷán-ɬkaxʷ‿kɬ
ta‿s.kíʕʷ-sw‿a." xʷuʔ, qʷacac-s-twit-as kʷúʔ‿x̌ɬ ʔá.kʷuʔ
ta‿s.cutáɬ-ih‿a, cixʷ-s-twít-as ʔá.kʷuʔ, n.q̇əlzaʔ-tn‿a lá.kʷuʔ,
xik-iṅ-ít-as‿kʷuʔ ʔayɬ ʔá.kʷuʔ n.q̇əlzaʔ-tn‿a, ciq-iṅ-ít-as‿kʷuʔ
ʔayɬ, cəq:ciq-iṅ-it-as‿kʷúʔ‿tuʔ, níɬ‿kʷuʔ‿x̌úʔ‿tuʔ ʔayɬ
s.zuqʷ-s ta‿s.cutáɬ‿a.

ʔá.tiʔ ɬ‿cəṁ-p-ás ta‿n.s.ptákʷɬ‿a. xʷʔáz‿həṁ‿tiʔ
kʷas‿wənáxʷ, s.ptákʷɬ‿tiʔ.

(7) ta‿s.qáyxʷ‿a ʔuḱ=íʾus-mín-tali ta‿míx̌aɬ‿a

ʔi‿xín̓-as, wáʔ‿kʷu? ta‿pá<pə>lʔ‿a s.qayxʷ, ta‿səmʔám-
s‿a, n.kə:kaɬás ʔi‿s.cm-áɬt-s‿a, l.kʷʔú-na n.x̌ʷís-tn‿a.
pápt‿kʷu? wa? ʔíʔwa? ɬwas‿píx̌əm̓ ʔi‿ḱsáytkən-s‿a,
xʷʔaz‿λ̓ú? kʷas‿ʔác̓x̌-əm kʷu‿s.tám̓, xʷʔaz kʷas‿zúqʷ-nuxʷ.
zúqʷ-nuxʷ‿kʷu? ʔi‿snəḱʷ:núḱʷaʔ-s‿a, kəɬ:kɬ-aẃs-n-ít-as
ʔi‿s.zuqʷ-nuxʷ-íh‿a, n.mi<mə>í̓-n-ít-as, xʷʔaz kʷas‿ʔúm̓-n-əm.

pálaʔ‿kʷu? ʔayɬ s.ʕap lá.ti? wa? s.ḱaí̓-əm-mín-əm
ʔə‿ki‿s.cm-áɬt-s‿a, niɬ s.huy̓-s ʔílal-wit ʔi‿s.cm-áɬt-s‿a,
táyt-wit. níɬ‿λ̓u? s.cún-tan-əm-wit ʔə‿ta‿s.kix-əzʔ-íh‿a:
"cúkʷ‿maɬ s.ʔílal-lap! ɬ‿λ̓íq-as ta‿s.qac-zaʔ-láp‿a, xʷʔit‿kɬ
kʷu‿s.ʔíɬən-lap."

pút‿ḱa‿λ̓u? λ̓íq-almən tiʔ‿ta‿s.qáyxʷ‿a, niɬ s.qan̓ím-s.
níɬ‿λ̓u? s.x̌aλ̓-s ta‿s.xʷákʷəkʷ-s‿a, qʷnúx̌ʷ-aɬc̓aʔ, níɬ‿λ̓u?
s.ṗəlḱ-ús-əm-s lá.ti?, niɬ s.qʷacác-s x̌áλ̓-əm ʔə‿ta‿sqʷəm‿a.

λ̓ak, x̌áλ̓-əm, cixʷ n.pəʕ:pʕ-ánk‿ti? ʔá.ta? s.qáyt-s‿a
tiʔ‿ta‿s.qʷəm‿a. wa? lá.ti? ta‿calaɬ‿a. niɬ s.lá.tiʔ-s ɬ‿ʕʷúy̓t-as.

ʕʷuy̓t lá.ti?, psii̓, niɬ s.qʷacác-s matq múta?, níɬ‿λ̓u?
səs‿ká.ti? matq-sút. wáʔ‿kʷu? cut: "húy̓-ɬkan‿λ̓u?
mátq‿λ̓u? λ̓u zúqʷ-kan, xʷʔaz kʷ‿ən.s.húz̓ ʔúx̌ʷai̓, húy̓-
ɬkan‿λ̓u? má<m̓>təq‿λ̓u? kən.cʔá-wna‿λ̓u?, zuqʷ-xən-
ɬkán‿kɬ λ̓u zúqʷ-kan."

λ̓ák‿kʷu? ká.ti?, niɬ s.ʔác̓x̌-n-as ta‿q̓ʷəx̌:q̓ʷíx̌-qʷ‿a míx̌aɬ
wa? s.mícaʔq ká.ti? n.kl-ús-c‿a. níɬ‿λ̓u? s.c̓itəm̓-mín-as,
xʷʔaz ká.ti? kʷas‿kəns.qʷús-xit-as. wa? sə́na? xʷʔit ʔi‿qʷəs-
m-áíc-s‿a, λ̓u? xʷʔaz ká.ti? kʷ‿s.qʷús-xit-as.

níɬ‿λ̓u? s.qʷai̓-út-s-tum̓ ʔə‿ta‿míx̌aɬ‿a: "tay, n.s.núḱʷa?,
ʔáma ta‿n.s.xʷákʷkʷ‿a t‿s.xʷʔáy-s‿a kʷasu‿qʷús-xi[t]-c.
wáʔ-ɬkan zəwát-ən ta‿waʔ‿s.zay-tən-s-túmih-as ʔi‿ḱsáytkən-
sw‿a. xʷʔay-s‿a‿λ̓ú?‿a kʷasu‿zúqʷ-nuxʷ, xʷʔaz kʷas‿ʔum̓-
ən-cíh-as-wit ɬwas‿zúqʷ-nuxʷ-wit. ɬ‿ʔiʔwaʔ-mín-c-axʷ,
ɬ‿s.zay-tən-mín-axʷ s.tám̓-as kʷu‿s.cún-cin, húy̓-ɬkan
cun-ám̓-ən-cin kʷa‿píx̌əm̓.

plán‿kʷuʔ waʔ ɬwálc-tən lá.tiʔ, niɬ s.cún-əm
ʔə‿ta‿míx̌aɬ‿a: "húy̓-ɬkaxʷ ʔiʔwaʔ-mín-c, húy̓-
ɬkaxʷ ʔul̓<=l̓>us-mín-c tákəm sútik." tiʔ‿ta‿míx̌aɬ‿a,
x̌zúm‿kʷuʔ‿tiʔ kʷu‿sk̓ʷ-álc-s lá.tiʔ l‿tsa‿wáʔ. pálaʔ l.t?ú-na
s.q̓ʷút-s‿a ta‿sk̓ʷ-álc-s‿a lá.tiʔ‿kʷuʔ ɬwas‿wác, l.tʔu mútaʔ
ta‿s.q̓ʷút‿a lá.tiʔ ɬwas‿kʷúṣaʔ, l.tʔu mútaʔ ta‿s.q̓ʷút‿a
wáʔ‿kʷuʔ lá.tiʔ n.x̌ak̓ʷ ta‿qʷúʔ‿a, qʷú<qʷu>ʔ, lá.tiʔ
ɬwas‿x̌íq ʔúqʷaʔ. "l.cʔa ɬwan‿wáʔ x̌u qapc, wáʔ-ɬkan
x̌áx̌-min̓-cin kʷ‿s.ʔul̓<=l̓>us-mín-c-axʷ."

níɬ‿kʷuʔ‿x̌uʔ s.txʷ-ús-əm-s ká.tiʔ ta‿s.qáyxʷ‿a, xʷʔaz
kʷ‿s.ʔác̓x̌-n-as ká.tiʔ kʷu‿s.tám̓, kʷu‿s.ʔíɬən. "s.tam-
as‿máɬ‿kɬ kʷu‿s.ʔíɬən-ɬkaɬ," wáʔ‿kʷuʔ n.cut-ánwas.
lá.tiʔ‿x̌uʔ, níɬ‿x̌uʔ s.zəwát-n-as ta‿míx̌aɬ‿a ɬ‿s.tám̓-as
ta‿waʔ‿s.ptínus-əm-s, níɬ‿kʷuʔ‿x̌uʔ s.cún-əm: "xʷʔaz
kʷasu‿ptínus-min kʷu‿s.ʔíɬən, wáʔ-ɬkan‿kɬ ʔúm̓-ən-cin
kʷu‿s.ʔíɬən."

níɬ‿x̌uʔ s.ká<kə>m̓-xal-s‿kʷuʔ? ʔayɬ ki‿qʷálc‿a ká.tiʔ,
k̓ʷúl̓-əm ta‿n.ʕʷúy̓t-tn‿a. x̌íl-əm‿kʷuʔ ta‿s.qáyxʷ‿a, q̓ix̌-
c-án̓-it-as tiʔ‿ta‿sk̓ʷ-álc‿a. "l.tʔu‿kɬ s.q̓ʷút‿a, lá.taʔ‿kɬ
ɬwaxʷ‿ʕʷúy̓t, l.cʔa‿kɬ s.ʔənc‿a," cút‿kʷuʔ.

"kəɬ-ən ̣maɬ ʔi ̣s.təṁ:tə́<tə>ṁ-sw ̣a." níɬ ̣kʷuʔ ̣x̌ʷuʔ ʔayɬ
s.ɬuq̓ʷ-uṅ-cút-s ta ̣s.qáyxʷ ̣a, kəɬ-n-ás ta ̣tə́x̌ʷʔac-s ̣a, kíc-
iṅ-as I.tʔú-na; niɬ s.kíc-ləx-s.

nəqʷ-álc ̣kʷuʔ, xʷʔaz ká.tiʔ kʷa ̣s.k̓ə́<k̓>x̌əṁ nukʷɬ
lá.tiʔ kʷas ̣ʔúɬxʷ. niɬ mútaʔ ta ̣súp̓-s ̣a ta ̣míx̌aɬ ̣a waʔ
ka.nuk̓ʷaʔ-s-tálih ̣a kʷas ̣wáʔ nəqʷ-álc. "xʷak-aṅ-cí-ɬkan ̣kɬ
ɬ ̣cíxʷ-as kʷ ̣s.húẏ-ɬkaɬ ʔíɬən," cút ̣kʷuʔ ta ̣míx̌aɬ ̣a.

cəṁ-p ̣kʷuʔ ʔá.tiʔ ta ̣x̌̓ánaṁ-tn ̣a, xʷák-aṅ-əṁ ̣kʷuʔ.
níɬ ̣x̌ʷuʔ s.xʷíċ-xit-əm ta ̣q̓út ̣a s.kʷakst x̌ix̌-al-akáʔ-əm
ká.tiʔ ta ̣míx̌aɬ ̣a. níɬ ̣x̌ʷuʔ s.cún-as: "I.kʷʔ-áwna xʷuy ċum-
ún cʔa ta ̣n.skʷákst ̣a." níɬ ̣x̌ʷuʔ s.ċuṁ-ún-as ta ̣s.kʷákst-s ̣a
ta ̣míx̌aɬ ̣a, ta ̣q̓ʷt-ákaʔ-s ̣a ʔayɬ mútaʔ ta ̣míx̌aɬ ̣a, níɬ ̣tiʔ
waʔ ċuṁ-ún-as s.niɬ. níɬ ̣tiʔ waʔ ta ̣waʔ ̣s.záy-tn-i x̌ʷʔúcin
x̌̓ánaṁ-tən.

qápc ̣kʷuʔ ʔayɬ, lis̓ʷ-c-áṅ-as ta ̣sk̓ʷ-álc ̣a tiʔ ̣ta ̣míx̌aɬ ̣a,
xʷiċ-xit-ə́m ̣kʷuʔ ta ̣tə́x̌ʷʔac-s ̣a, níɬ ̣x̌ʷuʔ s.zuh-um-cíṅ-əm-
n-əm.

kʷan-xit-ə́m ̣kʷuʔ ki ̣x̌ʷʔucin-álqʷ ̣a, ki ̣q̓ʷəs-m-álc-s ̣a,
níɬ ̣x̌ʷuʔ s.may-s-n-ás ̣ʔiž.

"kʷan ʔizá-wna," cún-əm ̣kʷuʔ. "ɬ ̣q̓ʷús-xit-axʷ
kʷu ̣s.táṁ, xʷʔaz ̣ʔiž kʷas ̣xík̓. xʷʔaz-as kʷasu ̣q̓ʷús-əm
kʷu ̣q̓ʷəx̌:q̓ʷíx̌-qʷ míx̌aɬ. xʷʔaz kʷu ̣s.xʷnáʔəm
kʷas ̣ka.xʷəna?m-an-cih-ás ̣a kʷ ̣s.xʷʔay-s kʷasu ̣zúqʷ-nuxʷ.
papt-káxʷ ̣kɬ ̣x̌ʷuʔ waʔ zúqʷ-nuxʷ ɬwaxʷ ̣píx̌əṁ. xʷʔaz
kʷas ̣húž tayt ʔi ̣k̓sáytkən-sw ̣a, ʔi ̣s.cm-ált-sw ̣a. kʷu ̣kə́laʔ
s.zúqʷ-nuxʷ-su, xʷʔaz-as kʷ ̣s.ʔúṁ-n-axʷ kʷu ̣s.wát,
cúkʷ ̣x̌ʷuʔ ʔi ̣k̓sáytkən-sw ̣a, ta ̣səm?ám-sw ̣a mútaʔ
ʔi ̣s.cm-ált-sw ̣a." níɬ ̣kʷuʔ ̣x̌ʷuʔ ʔayɬ s.q̓ʷál-n-əm
n.káʔ-as ̣kɬ ɬwas ̣pún-as ʔi ̣cíʔ ̣a.

niɬ s.q̓ʷacác-s tiʔ ̣ta ̣s.qáyxʷ ̣a, x̌̓ák ̣kʷuʔ ̣x̌ʷuʔ, cixʷ
ʔə ̣ta ̣s.x̌ək-xít-m ̣a ʔə ̣ta ̣míx̌aɬ ̣a, q̓ʷús-xit-as ta ̣xzúm ̣a
s.x̌ʷláxkən. niɬ s.kʷán-as, niɬ s.k̓ih-k-míṅ-as ʔayɬ, niɬ
s.ʔúx̌ʷal-s-as. x̌̓ak kən.tʔú kʷu ̣s.xáʔ-s ̣a I ̣ta ̣s.wáʔ-s ̣a
ʔiž ̣ʔi ̣núkʷ ̣a ʔúxʷalmixʷ, ká.tiʔ ̣kʷuʔ ɬ ̣x̌̓ák-as. cixʷ ʔá.tiʔ

ta‿səm?ám-s‿a, I‿tsa‿wá?. plan wa? x̌a⟨x̌ə⟩íʾ-qʷ-ám̓‿kʷu?
ta‿səm?ám-s‿a, cut kʷ‿s.plan-s wa? s.zá?tən. tákəm sútik
kʷ‿s.xʷ?ay-s kʷ‿s.wa?-s ta‿kʷtámc-s‿a, nił s.cut-s
kʷ‿s.plán-s‿tu? wa? zuqʷ.

níł‿ƛ̓u? s.ċaqʷ-an̓-ít-as ti?‿ta‿ċí?‿a s.ƛ̓íq-xal-s, ƛ̓iq
?áċx̌-n-əm ?ə‿ki‿núkʷ‿a ?úxʷalmixʷ, xʷ?az kʷ‿s.?um̓-
n-ás‿?iż kʷu‿s.tám̓. níł‿kʷu?‿ƛ̓u? s.qlíl-i, cút-wit‿kʷu?:
"cil-kst ƛ̓ánam̓-tən kʷ‿s.xʷ?ay-s kʷas‿ƛ̓íq, pə⟨p⟩la[?]-?úl
ċi? ta‿s.ƛ̓íq-xal-s‿a. plán‿ƛ̓u? wa? ?áma kʷ‿s.pal?-ac-min̓-
as‿ƛ̓ú?‿ti?, ċaqʷ-an̓-ás‿ƛ̓u? s.nił."

qʷacác‿kʷu? múta? píx̌əm̓, ?úḯ⟨=íʾ⟩us-n-as ?i‿ċí?‿a
I‿ta‿pal?-úlm̓əxʷ‿a lá.ti?, nił s.zúqʷ-s-as tákəm. x̌ʷ?úcin
kʷ‿s.q̓ə́⟨q̓ə⟩m̓p-s ċi? ?i‿zúqʷ-s-as‿a. kʷí⟨kʷ⟩s‿kʷu?‿ƛ̓u?
łlá.ti? ta‿s.kʷám-s‿a, níł‿?iż ?úx̌ʷal-s-as. "?u, qʷən:qʷán-t
ta‿s.qáyxʷ‿a," cún-əm‿kʷu? ?ə‿ki‿núkʷ‿a ?úxʷalmixʷ,
"zúqʷ-nuxʷ‿k̓a núkʷun̓‿a, kʷi⟨kʷ⟩s ta‿s.ƛ̓íq-xal-s‿a."
qʷacác-wit‿kʷu? ?aył píx̌əm̓ wi‿s.níł, ƛ̓ák-wit, xʷ?áy‿ƛ̓u?
kʷ‿s.zúqʷ-nuxʷ-i, cúkʷ‿ƛ̓u? ta‿s.ƛ̓al-ál-ih‿a.

wá?‿kʷu? ta‿pá⟨pə⟩l?‿a qəłmə́⟨mə⟩n̓ I‿wi‿s.níł,
níł‿kʷu?‿ƛ̓u? s.cut-s: "zəwat=ət-s-ás‿ti? kʷa‿píx̌əm̓, wá?‿ƛ̓u?
zəwát-n-as n.ká?-as łwas‿wá? ?i‿ċí?‿a. ł‿?ámh-as kʷ‿s.qʷal̓-
út-s-alap, s.x̌ək ?um̓-ən-tumuł-ás‿kł."

wá?‿ƛ̓u? ?áył‿ƛ̓u? qʷacác-wit‿ƛ̓u? ?aył tákəm.
Gee‿kʷu? ?aył, ?i‿cíxʷ-wit-as, s.x̌áw‿ti?‿ƛ̓u?, ?aċx̌-n-ít-as,
s.łə́k‿ƛ̓u? ?i‿ċí?‿a. suq̓ʷ-əm-wít‿kʷu? ?aył lá.ti?, pála? s.qit,
put, ʕap, psil múta? ta‿núkʷ‿a s.qit. pút‿ƛ̓u? múta?
ʕap, ta‿núkʷ‿a s.qit lá.ti? ł‿qʷəmƛ̓-s-twít-as ?i‿ċí?‿a.

nił s.tə́x̌ʷ-s‿ƛ̓u? ?aył x̌ʷəy-s-túm ?ə‿ki‿n.k̓sáytkən-s‿a.
ʕəl:ʕəl kʷu‿s.qáyxʷ, ?á⟨?⟩x̌a? kʷa‿píx̌əm̓.

Nilh Izá Sptákwlhkalh
● ● ● ● ● ● ● ● ● ● ● ● ● ● ● ●
These Are Our Legends

1.

I á7eṅwasa nk̇yap

The Two Coyotes

TOLD BY BILL EDWARDS

(1) I á7eṅwasa nk̓yap

Tak ku7 káti7 i nk̓yápa, á7eṅwas. Nilh ku7 tu7 stsut.s ta pépel7a lhlak iż: "Nk̓yáplhkan, tákem tu7 swat wa7 zewatentsálitas kwenswá nk̓yap. K̓a malh cw7aoz snúwa kwásu nk̓yap, pepla7lhkácw."

"Cw7aoz káti7, nk̓yápkan tu7 tit," tsut ku7.

"Cw7aoz káti7, pepla7lhkácw. Cuy malh zaṁ, húy̓lhkacw zewáten lhkúnsa. Húy̓lhkan taq̓ lts7áwna lta nlep̓cáltna, k̓alaṅmiṅlhkácw tu7 i ucwalmícwa."

Taq̓ ku7 aylh, taq̓ ku7 áti7, atsxném ku7 eki ucwalmícwa. "Tay, tak kent7ú ta nk̓yápa, nk̓yap káti7 ta táka." Tak ku7, kacíṁa ku7 tu7.

Qwatsáts ku7 aylh lhelkw7ú ni7 na núkwa, kalhéxwa ku7 tu7, qwaxtminitás ku7.

"Tak múta7 káti7 ta pépel7a, pépla7 káti7 ta táka múta7."

Tak ku7, tsicw ku7 aylh, pzánas ku7 na snúk̓wa7sa.

"Á7hantsu," tsúnem ku7, "á7hantsu, qaṅimenswítkacw ha? Nk̓yáplhkan, pepla7lhkácw snúwa."

(1) The Two Coyotes

Two coyotes were going along. Then one of them said, "I am a coyote, everybody knows that I am a coyote. But you are not a coyote, you are 'another one.'"

"No way, I am also a coyote," the other one said.

"Not at all, you are 'another one.' Okay, you will know it right now. I am going to go across this garden, you listen to the people."

Well, he went across, and while he was going across he was seen by the people. "Hey, there is a coyote going there, it is a coyote that is going there." He carried on, and he went out of sight.

Then the other one took off, he suddenly appeared, and they noticed him.

"There goes another one, it's another one that is going there."

He carried on, and he got to the other spot, where he met his friend.

"See?" he was told, "See? did you hear them? I am a coyote, but you are 'another one.'"

2.

Weq̇w ti nk̇yápa

Coyote Drowns

TOLD BY ROSIE JOSEPH

(2) Weq̓w ti nk̓yápa

Húy̓lhkan aylh ucwalmícwtsmiṅ lts7áwna ti nk̓yápa. Stexw ti7 scéceṁ. Ṫak ku7 káta7, cá7sa et7úna ti qú7a. Súxwast, úqwa7, ṫak múta7 xáṫem.

Wa7 ṫu7 áti7 xílem, nilh ṫu7 skí7keis kwas xáṫem. Nilh ṫu7 múta7 s7áta7s xaẇxaẇxáẇna lhṫákas lhá7sa ṫú7a ti qú7a; ṫak ku7 káti7. Plan múta7 úqwa7, plan múta7.

Tsáma ṫu7, nilh ṫu7 scw7ays kw scáṫlecs. Ṫak aylh l ti qú7a. Tsukw ṫu7 i sq̓wáxtsa wa7 smul.

Ṫak ṫu7, lan múta7 úqwa7. Tsáma ṫu7, nilh ṫu7 slans ṫu7 múta7 wa7 ṫak qemp ti sq̓íta, nilh ṫu7 múta7 skék7aẇs áta7 ti stáksa.

Áti7 aylh gwelínsa lhwas kamulmulmúla l ti qú7a, gwelínsa. Plan múta7 úqwa7.

Ṫak ṫu7, nilh ṫu7 selts7ás kwṫústsa lhtsícwalmenas ti qú7a. Kwikws ṫu7 aylh láti7 kwas múltsaṁ, lan úqwa7, úqwa7.

Wa7 ṫu7 áti7 xílem ṫu weq̓w tu7 ṫu7, nilh k̓a tu7 ṫu7 szuqws.

(2) Coyote Drowns

I am going to tell a story about this coyote in Indian. He was really silly. He was going along there, a ways up from the water. He went down, he had a drink, and he went uphill again.

He kept doing that until he got too lazy to go uphill. So he stayed all the way down, while he was going along close to the water; and he just kept on going. Well, he had another drink, and another one.

After a while he didn't even have the energy to get out any more. He just kept going along in the water. Only his feet were in the water.

So he went on, he had another drink. The going was getting tough, and pretty soon the day was getting hotter, so he went in a little bit further.

All the way he was up to his stomach in the water, up to his stomach. And he drank some more.

He kept on going, so the water came up to his face. He just dipped his mouth a little bit into the water, and he was already drinking, drinking.

He kept on doing that until he got carried away by the water, and he died, I guess.

3.

Ta nk'yápa múta7 ta tsúquma

Coyote and Chickadee

TOLD BY BILL EDWARDS

(3) Ta nk̓yápa múta7 ta tsúqum̓a

Nk̓yap ti7 múta7 ts7áwna ku sptakwlh. Zact ti7 séna7 t̓u7, lhq̓íq̓at t̓u7 ta wa7 zewátnan.

T̓ak ku7 káti7 ta nk̓yápa, atsxnás ku7 ta tsúqum̓a wa7 káti7. "Wá7lhkacw kánem?," tsúnas ku7 ta tsúqum̓a.

"U, wá7lhkan píxem̓."

Atsxcítas ku7 ta téxw7atssa. "U," tsúnas ku7, "Stam̓ kelh láti7 kwa zúqwsacw l ta téxw7atsswa? Kwikws7úl, kwikws7úl! Cw7aoz láti7 kwásu zuqws ku stam̓."

"Cuy qa7 zam̓, nas et7úna x7ílha áti7 l ta nlep̓cáltna, xwem t̓u7 láti7 kw sqam̓tstúmin lhelts7á."

"Cuy," tsut ku7 ta nk̓yápa, nilh ku7 staks áta7, tsicw ku7 áta7 x7ílha. Nilh t̓u7 tu7 slhápnas lhwas kánem, nilh t̓u7 káti7 swa7s pu7y̓acwám.

Kwilqscítem ku7 aylh lhelt7ú lhel ta tsúqum̓a, klhaka7cítem ku7 áti7, put t̓u7 qám̓tstum̓; q̓mínnem ku7 láti7, nilh szuqws.

Nilh ku7 láti7 ti7 skitss, tákem ta sútika, qapts. [..]

T̓ak ku7 káti7 ta snúk̓wa7sa. "Tay, stám̓as k̓a núkun̓ ku száytensu. Cw7aoz hem̓ t̓u7 kw scw7ays kw száytenlhkacw kwásu wa7 láti7 skits."

Q̓elcan7aném ku7, q̓elcan7aném ku7, xw7útsin kw sq̓elcán7anem.

Tcúsem ku7, tík̓lec ku7 aylh. "U, lts7a k̓a núkun̓ lhgúy̓tan," tsut ku7. Plan ku7 wa7 kalhmv́ka i t̓áminsa. "Lts7a k̓a lhgúy̓tan," tsut ku7.

Húhu7 múta7 séna7 lhelts7áwna, zact ti7 ts7a ku sptakwlh t̓u7. Tsukw t̓u7 ta wa7 zewátnan.

(3) Coyote and Chickadee

This is another *sptakwlh* about Coyote. It is supposed to be long, but I only know a short part of it.

Well, Coyote was going along, and he saw Chickadee who was around there. "What are you up to?" he asked Chickadee.

"Oh, I'm hunting."

Then he saw Chickadee's bow. "Oh," he said to him, "What are you going to kill with that bow of yours? It's too small, it's too small! You won't kill anything with that."

"All right, you go that way, to the other side of that garden, and I'll hit you from there, for sure." [said Chickadee]

"Okay," said Coyote, and he went to the other side. But then he forgot what he was doing, and he started to hunt mice.

But Chickadee took aim at him, he let go, and he hit him; Coyote fell down, and he died.

So he laid there all winter till spring.

Then, one day his friend came by. "Say, you must have done something again. It can't be that you have not done something that you are lying there."

He jumped over him, he jumped over him, four times he jumped over him.

Coyote looked up, and he stretched himself. "Oh, I must have slept here," he said. His fur was already coming off rotting. "I must have slept here," he said.

Well, it goes on from here, this is a long *sptakwlh*. But this is all I know of it.

4.

Ti nk̓yápa múta7 ti skalúl7a

Coyote and Owl

TOLD BY ROSIE JOSEPH

(4) Ti nk̓yápa múta7 ti skalúl7a

Wa7 ku7 lts7a ti nk̓yápa. Wa7 xát̓miṅas kwas ka7átṡxma lhas sit.st. Plan ku7 aylh wa7 gápalmen; wa7 em7ímnem ti skalúl7a. Nilh t̓u7 stsúnas: "Tay, Skalula7, kánem ses xzum i nkwt̓ústeṅswa?"

Nilh t̓u7 stsut.s ti skalúl7a: "Nilh kwenswá ka7átṡxma lhas sit.st," tsut ku7. "U," tsut ku7 ti nk̓yápa, "Wá7lhkan t̓it xát̓miṅ kwenswá ka7átṡxma lhas sit.st, xílem snúwa. Wá7lhkacw kasts, nilh t̓u7 ses xzum i nkwt̓ústeṅswa?"

"U," tsut ku7 ti skalúl7a, "lhxát̓miṅacw kwas xzum i nkwt̓ústeṅswa, nilh t̓u7 snástsu kwam ku qwal̓ílh. Wá7lhkacw t̓u7 zewáten i qwal̓íha, kéla7 q̓ix. Meqwenskacw, nilh t̓u7 sqiqtṡmínacw. Qiqtṡmínlhkacw láti7 t̓u plan t̓u7 wa7 lil̓q kwas katsésa. Alaskácw t̓u7 qíqtṡmin, nilh t̓u7 s7ámas, nilh t̓u7 stṡemq̓ánacw, nilh t̓u7 stṡeq̓pánacw l ti nkwt̓ústeṅswa ti núkwa, tṡíla ti núkwa, nilh t̓u7 stṡílas t̓u7 áti7. Kelhenlhkácw, plan kelh xzum i nkwt̓ústeṅswa."

"Cuy nas," tsut, nilh ku7 t̓u7 st̓aks ti nk̓yápa. T̓ak, kwam ku7 i qwal̓ílha, qíqtṡem ku7 aylh láti7 t̓u plan t̓u7 aylh wa7 lil̓q kwas katsésa láti7 ti sqíqtṡsa. Tṡemq̓ánas ku7 aylh, nilh t̓u7 slhúmunas l ti nkwt̓ústeṅsa, tṡeq̓pánas. Wa7 ku7 aylh láti7 steqsás t̓u kaguy̓tá t̓u7.

My, stexw t̓u7 qvl ti sxílemsa. Kanmás k̓a; cw7ay t̓u7 kw szewátnan tṡílhas nka7 kw sciṅs kw sguy̓t.s. Cwak, lan k̓ac ti sqíqtṡsa. Nilh t̓u7 swa7s láti7 kelhnás, tsáma kelhnás, cw7ay t̓u7 kwas kaxílha, plan t̓u7 wa7 k̓ac.

Qaṅimensás ku7 aylh ti skalúl7a, lánsa aylh múta7 wa7 gápalmen. "Kalúla7," tsúnas, "kánem su xílhtum̓x ets7á? Átṡxen, tṡeq̓p aylh i qwal̓ílha l ti nkwt̓ústṅa."

"U," tsut ku7 ti skalúl7a, tsuwa7sú t̓u7 száyten. Kánem múta7 sacw guy̓t?"

(4) Coyote and Owl

Here was Coyote. He wanted to be able to see at night. It was already getting dark; Owl was hooting. So he said to Owl: "Hey, Owl, why are your eyes so big?"

So Owl said: "So I can see at night," that's what he said. "Oh," Coyote said, "I want to be able to see at night too, just like you. What do you do to make your eyes so big?"

"Oh," Owl said, "if you want your eyes to be big, you go and get some pitch. You know what pitch is, it is really hard. Put it in your mouth and chew it. Chew it until it is easy to stretch. You chew it really well, so it will be good, then you break it apart, you stick one piece on one eye and the other piece on the other eye, and you leave it like that. You take it off, and your eyes will be big."

"Go now," he said, so Coyote went. He went and got some pitch, and he chewed it there till it was easy to stretch, that stuff he had been chewing. He broke it in half and he put it on his eyes, he stuck it on. So he was holding it there till he fell asleep.

My, it was too bad what happened to him. One way or the other he overslept; I don't know how long he slept, but when he woke up, the stuff he had been chewing was already dry. So he tried really hard to take it off, but it didn't work, it was already dry.

Then he heard Owl, because it was already getting dark again. "Owl," he said, "why did you do this to me? Look, the pitch got stuck in my eyes."

"Oh," said Owl, "it is your own fault. Why did you sleep?"

"Cw7aoz qa7 séna7 kwenswá guẏt, meskán t̓u7 kaguẏtá t̓u7."

"Á7han, tsuwa7sú t̓u7 száyten!," tsúnem, "lhcw7áozas ka kw sgúẏt.su, lan ka tu7 wa7 xzum i nkwt̓ústeṅswa. Á7han, tśilawílc aylh múta7 i nkwt̓ústeṅswa, wa7 t̓u7 qwiqws."

Tsukw ti7 t̓u7.

"I wasn't going to sleep, but I fell asleep after all."

"See, it is your own fault," Owl told him, "if you hadn't slept, your eyes would have been big. But look now, your eyes are the same size again, they are small."

That's all.

5.

Ti s̓talhálama múta7
i stsmáĺt.sa i míxalha

Grizzly Bear
and Black Bear's Children

TOLD BY ADELINA WILLIAMS

(5) Ti stalhálama múta7 i stsmált.sa i míxalha

Wa7 kémem i míxalha, ti sqatsez7íha múta7 ti skicez7íha; nilh ses huż. Lhwalnítas i stsmaltíha l ti s7á7tseqsa ti srápa.

Wa7 ku7 káti7 ti stalhálama, púnas i skwemkúkwmita, nilh tu7 scelhantsút.s kwas huż álkwilh.

Wa7 aylh láti7 álkwilh, tiq ku7 i míxalha.

Tsut ku7: "Wá7lhkan lts7a alkwentánihan wi stsetsewqínkst. Áma, áma t.sálapa wa7 káku7 gelílc, naskaláp tu7 múta7. Alkwilhkán kelh, kukwcitumulhkán kelh."

Qwatsáts ku7 ka tu7 i wa7 estsmált, nilh tu7 slans kwánas, nlhamánas ku7 e ti ntsqústna i á7eńwasa skwemkúkwmit, kúkuńas. Tiq ku7 i wa7 estsúwa7, huż ku7 tsut: "Plánlhkan qwels láti7 i húża s7ílhenlap. Wa7 malh wá7wi, wa7 malh wá7wi!"

Nilh ku7 tu7 láti7 stsa7cws i míxalha, ti slánsa wa7 qwel i húża s7ílhni, nilh ku7 stsut.s: "Wá7lhkan hem kelh tu7 lts7a, wa7 malh wá7wi!"

Nilh ku7 aylh kela7úl nlhámcal ti sqátsez7a míxalh, wa7 xílhtsas ets7á, nílhas ku7 ti skwékwza7sa tsetsewqínkst.

"U, kw swéta7," tsunitás ku7, nílha cwilh ka i stsmaltkálha sqwelcitúmulhas." Kwanitás ku7 láti7 i wa7 skwilh skwezkwékwez7i, nilh ku7 tu7 sqwatsátsi.

Ts7as ku7 aylh kálim ti stalhálama qelqeltsín kw scw7ays kwas lhwal. Áku7 tsícwwit ku7 e ti srápa, nilh tu7 stkíwleci. Wa7 ku7 láti7 sqwem i scúcwża l ti s7a7tseqsá ti7 ti srápa.

Cw7aoz ku7 tu7 aylh kw scińs, tiq ku7 aylh ti stalhálama. "Cuy malh cuy lháku7, tsaqmińi kw stsetsewqínkst, kateqskaná kelh lts7a xáwńa."

(5) Grizzly Bear and Black Bear's Children

There were some Black Bears digging roots, a father and a mother with their cubs; they had found a spot where they were going to stay for a while. So they left their children at the bottom of a tree.

But Grizzly Bear was around there, she found the children, and she took it upon herself to babysit for them.

So she was babysitting, when the Black Bears came back.

So Grizzly said: "I am babysitting for these cubs. It is good, it is good that you are working so hard, so go again. I will babysit, and I will cook for you folks."

Well, the parents took off, and then Grizzly took the two children, put them in the pot and cooked them. When the parents came back, she told them: "I already cooked something for you folks to eat. Go ahead, go ahead!"

Well, the Black Bears were glad that their food had been cooked already, and Grizzly said: "I am just going to stay here, but you folks go right ahead!"

So the father bear was the first one to serve himself, he was just doing that, and then it turned out that it was his own cub.

"Oh, that Grizzly," they said, "it is our own children that she cooked for us." They took the children, which had been left over, and they went away.

Grizzly came along too, following them and begging not to be left behind. The Black Bears got to a tree, and they climbed it. There was a big anthill at the bottom of that tree.

Not before long Grizzly came. "Come on now, you guys, throw down a cub, I'll catch it here below."

"U, kaṫíla ṫú7a ka7lh, kaṫíla," tsúnem ku7, "mítsa7q láti7 lti sqwéma. Láti7 lh7utszílcacw, nilh kelh áta7 stŝaq́miṅcítsim kw stsetseẇqíṅkst. Utszílcacw, npiġwqáṁlhkacw."

Xílem ku7 aylh tsáẇtswa láti7; mítsa7q ku7 l ti cucwżálhcwa. "Cuy malh, lánlhkan aylh wa7 s7útsez."

"Ḱálem ṫu7 ka7lh, utszílc ka7lh; xílhtskacw ets7á i skwákst.swa, npiġwqáṁlhkacw, nilh kelh ṫu7 scw7ays kw skelhpaka7mínacw kw stsetseẇqíṅkst."

Xílem ku7 aylh áti7, npiġwqáṁ ku7, xílhtsas ku7 ets7á i skwákst.sa.

Wa7s ku7 láti7 qeİqeİtsíṅ kw slans wa7 skwiİ, cw7aoz ku7 ṫu7 kwas tŝaq́miṅcítem lhláti7 i sḱwemḱúḱwṁita. Tsunitás ku7 kwas gelílc kwas npíġwqaṁ.

Cw7aoz ku7 ṫu7 aylh kw sciṅs, lan ku7 aylh ulhcwmínem e ki scúcwża.

Huż ku7 aylh tsut: "Ananáh, ananáh, wáytkan lákw7a, ananáh, wáytkan."

"U, kaṫíla ṫú7a, álas npíġwqaṁ. Tseq.wálaka7 ets7áwna, tŝaq́miṅém kelh áta7 kw stsetseẇqíṅkst."

Wa7 ku7 ṫu7 aylh: "Ananáh, ananáh."

Zikt ku7 tu7 ṫu7 aylh, lans ku7 ḱa aylh ntŝaqwqáṅem e ki scúcwża.

Tsukw ti7.

"Oh, take it easy, take it easy," they told her, "sit down on that pile. Sit down firmly, and we'll throw a cub to you. Fix yourself, and open your bum."

So that's what the poor thing did; she sat down on the anthill. "Okay, I'm all set."

"Wait a minute, fix yourself; hold your hands like this, and open your bum, so you won't miss the cub."

Well, that's what she did, she opened her bum, and she held her hands the way she had been told to do.

She was nagging them that she was ready, but still they didn't throw her the children. They told her to open her bum really wide.

It didn't take long before the ants entered her.

So she said: "Ananáh, ananáh, something is wrong with me, ananáh, something is wrong with me."

"Oh, just keep still, open your bum really wide. Hold your arms up this way and we'll throw you a cub."

Well, she really had a hard time: "Ananáh, ananáh."

Finally she keeled over, as the ants had already eaten her bum.

That's all.

6.

Ta sm'ém'lhatsa múta7 ta skalúl7a

The Girl and the Owl

TOLD BY MARTINA LAROCHELLE

(6) Ta sḿéḿlhatsa múta7 ta skalúl7a

Húẏlhkan ptakwlh, ptákwlhmin lts7a ta sḿéḿlhatsa, wa7 ílal l ta s7ístkna. Wa7 ku7 ílal láti7 ta sḿéḿlhatsa, cw7ay t̓u7 kwas katékwa. Nilh ku7 t̓u7 stsut.s ta kwékwa7sa: "Cw7áozas kwásu katékwa, nilh t̓u7 nshuż xlíten ta skalúl7a, ts7asmiṅtsíhas kelh ta skalúl7a."

Cw7ay t̓u7 kwas katékwa, stáḿas k̓a malh kwa ilalmínas ta sk̓úk̓wḿita, ta sḿéḿlhatsa. Plan ku7 ti7 wa7 aṅwaszánucw k̓a, kalhaszánucw k̓a ti7 ti wa7 ílal.

Cw7ay t̓u7 kwas katékwa, nilh ku7 t̓u7 stsut.s ta kwékwa7sa: "U, huż xlítnem ta skalúl7a, huż ts7asmiṅtsíhas."

Cw7ay t̓u7 kwas katékwa, nilh ku7 t̓u7 aylh stsut.s ta kwékwa7sa: "Sima7mín malh lts7a ta wa7 ílal, cw7ay t̓u7 kwas katékwa, sima7mín malh, Skalúla7."

Cw7aoz ku7 t̓u7 láti7 kw sciṅs, put, ts7as ku7 t̓elh ta skalúl7a. "Huhú hu, ts7ásmiṅlhkan kw sKíka7," tsut ku7 ta skalúl7a.

"Síma7 t̓u7, síma7, sima7mín t̓u7."

"Huhú hu, ts7ásmiṅlhkan kw sKíka7," tsut ku7 ta skalúl7a. Cw7aoz ku7 t̓u7 láti7 kw sciṅs, t̓épa kú7a ta s7ístkna, nílha cwilh k̓a lh7úlhcwas ta skalúl7a ta s7ístkna lhelt7ú nlhá7ctna lhelt.sa úlhcwwit i ucwalmícwa.

Lhláti7 lh7úlhcwas ta skalúl7a. Cw7aoz ku7 t̓u7 aylh múta7 kw sciṅs, kat̓ék̓a ku7 tu7 aylh ta sk̓úk̓wḿita, splánsa cwilh aylh kwánem tu7 e ti skalúl7a.

Nlaḿánas ku7 aylh láti7 l ta tŝlá7sa, qul láti7 i naxwíta, i scúcwża, i takmá t̓u7 láti7, i p̓egp̓íġlhha, qul ku7 t̓u7 l ti tŝlá7sa, nlhaḿqáṅas ku7 aylh láti7 ta sḿéḿlhatsa.

50

(6) The Girl and the Owl

I am going to tell a *sptakwlh*, a *sptakwlh* about this girl who was crying in the underground house. The girl was crying there, and she would not hush.

So her grandmother said: "If you don't hush, I will call the Owl, the Owl will come for you."

She would not hush, whatever the child, the little girl, was crying for. I guess she was about two or three years old, the one that was crying.

She would not hush, so her grandmother said: "Oh, we'll call for the Owl, he will come for you."

She did not hush, so her grandmother said: "Come here for the one who is crying, she won't hush, so come and get her, Owl."

It didn't take long before the Owl came. "Hoohoo hoo, I have come to get Kíka7," said the Owl.

"Come then, come, come and get her."

"Hoohoo hoo, I have come to get Kíka7," said the Owl. It didn't take long before it got dark in the underground house, because the Owl entered the underground house coming down the ladder on which the people enter.

That is where the Owl entered. Pretty soon the girl stopped crying, because the Owl had already taken her.

He put her in his basket, which was full of snakes, ants, everything, frogs, his basket was full of them, and he put the girl right in there, on the bottom.

T̓u7 snilhts aylh sqwatsátss, úxwal̓sas ku tsitcws k̓a ti7 ta skalúl7a. K̓a lhwas estsítcw, k̓a lhstám̓as ken kwas káku7, ta sáẇta. Wa7 ku7 aylh láti7, nilh t̓u7 aylh ses m7ámminas ta sm̓ém̓lhatsa, m7amminás ku7 aylh láti7. Ts7as ku7 t̓elh ta sm̓ém̓lhatsa, ts7as ku7 t̓elh, tṡíla qa7eżmínas ta skalúl7a lhwas k̓ul̓tsáṅem, t̓íqcitem i sqweyítsa, i staġésezha, i sm̓úmtm̓a, i takmá t̓u7. Cw7aoz kwas zewátnas lhwas kas lhwas q̓wel. Cw7aoz múta7 kw skatṡáqwsasa lhwas xí7xeẇ.

Wa7 ku7 aylh, wa7 ku7 káti7 ta stsitsá7a.

"Síma7 qa7 ets7á, síma7 ets7á, húẏlhkan ksnántsin," tsúnas ku7 ta stsitsá7a.

T̓u7 snilhts aylh sksnánas, sqwál̓nas aylh ta stsitsá7a ku huẏ száytens lhtsícwas áku7 úxwal̓ e ki s7ístkna, e ki slal̓íl̓tem̓sa. Nilh t̓u7 stsúnas ku7 ta stsitsá7a: "Húẏlhkacw nas, kwáncits ku cwik̓áż, ku zút̓smen, mek̓ilólya7," tsut wi7. Stám̓as k̓a wi7 múta7 kwelh wa7 mek̓ilólya7, cw7aoz kwenswá zewáten, meskán t̓u7 wa7 tsut "mek̓ilólya7;" "mek̓ilólya7," tsut ku7.

"U," tsut ku7 t̓elh ta stsitsá7a, "u," qwatsáts ku7 t̓elh ta stsitsá7a áku7 e ki slal̓íl̓tem̓sa ti7 ta sm̓ém̓lhatsa. Qwatsáts ku7, nilh ku7 t̓u7 staks, t̓ak ku7 ta stsitsá7a áti7 s7ístkna, l ki wa7 estsítcw.

"Ah, ah," tsut ku7 t̓u7 ta stsitsá7a, "ts7asmiṅcítkan sKíka7 i mek̓ilólya7sa, cwik̓áẏsa, zút̓smensa, ah, ah," tsut ku7 aylh ta stsitsá7a.

"U saẇt, síma7 t̓u7, síma7 t̓u7." Qaṅím k̓a wi7 káti7 kwelh wa7 estsítcw, qaṅím. "Síma7 t̓u7, síma7 t̓u7, saẇt."

Nilh ku7 t̓u7 múta7 stsut.s t̓u7: "Ts7asmiṅcítkan sKíka7 i cwik̓áẏsa, mek̓ilólya7sa, zút̓smensa." U saẇt, u saẇt.

"Síma7 t̓u7." Kwánas ku7 aylh káti7 i cwik̓áża, mek̓ilóley7a, i..wéna7..zút̓smensa. "U, qwatsáts malh."

And then the Owl took off, and he brought her to his house. I guess he had some kind of house, whatever it was that he had there, the poor fellow.

That is where he lived, and he kept the girl as a wife, he kept her there. But the girl got sort of tired of the Owl, because of the kind of food he brought her: rabbits, squirrels, grouse, all those things. She did not know how it was cooked. And she could not eat it while it was still raw.

But the Crow happened to be around there.

"Come here, please, come here, I will send you on an errand," she told the Crow.

So she sent the Crow on his errand, and she told him what to do when he would get to the underground house, to her parents. She said to the Crow: "You will go and get me some prepared salmon, paint, and *mek̓ilólya7*, she said. Whatever *mek̓ilólya7* is, I don't know, but I say *mek̓ilólya7*; "*mek̓ilólya7*," she said.

"Oh," said the Crow, "oh," and he took off to the parents of the girl. He took off and he went to the underground house, to the people who were living there.

"Aeh, aeh," said the Crow, "I have come for Kika7's *mek̓ilólya7*, for her prepared salmon, her paint, aeh, aeh," said the Crow.

"Oh, poor guy, come in, come in." Apparently the people who were living there had heard him. "Come in, come in, poor thing."

Again he said: "I have come to get Kika7's prepared salmon, her *mek̓ilólya7*, her paint." Oh, poor thing, poor thing.

"Come in." He took the prepared salmon, the *mek̓ilólya7*, and her..uhm..paint. "Oh, go now."

Qwatsátssas ku7 iż, tsícwsas ku7 aylh áku7 e ti skalúl7a, láku7 ltsa wá7sas ta sṁéṁlhatsa. Wa7 k̓a wi7 múta7 zewátnas ku tsitcws ta skalúl7a.

Wa7 ku7 aylh láti7 ptínusem ku7 ta smúlhatsa lhhúżas kánem, nilh t̓u7 shuẏs lhláti7 q̓áylec. Meysantsút ku7 aylh, tsicw ku7 múta7, kwánas i síkila, tákma káti7. Tákem ku7 t̓u7 kw swíṅacws i stsícwa kw sk̓ul̓s ta sṁéṁlhatsa. Huẏ ti7 láti7 máysnas ta kwtámtssa, nilh t̓u7 shuẏs q̓áylec lhláti7.

Wa7 ku7, plan ku7 tu7 ti7 aylh qwatsáts píxeṁ ta skalúl7a, cwíl̓em ku sqweyíts muta7 ku tákem t̓u7 káti7 wa7 t̓u7 t̓íqsas: i sṁúṁtṁa, i staġésezha, t̓íqcitas ta skíġwsa, nilh ti7 aylh wa7 nahnás kwa skiġw. Stáṁas k̓a malh ti7, cw7aoz kwenswa zewáten lhstáṁas kwa skiġw.

Cw7aoz múta7 kwas xekcítsas na nkwékw7a lhstáṁas kwa skiġw. Nilh k̓a wi7 heṁ ta sem7amminása ta sṁéṁlhatsa.

Wa7 ku7 aylh láti7 ptínusem ta sṁéṁlhatsa lhhúżas kánem, nilh t̓u7 skaq̓áylecsa. Tsut ku7: "U, húẏlhkan nas cwíl̓em ku síkil." Kwánas ku7 i síkila káti7, i qwal̓ílha, i takmá t̓u7.

Cuy, ts7as ku7 t̓elh ta skalúl7a, t̓iq ku7.

"Síma7 t̓u7, ápa7, síma7 t̓u7." Plans aylh wa7 meysantsút, huż úxwal̓. "Nleq̓wlaq̓walúsem malh," tsúnas ku7 aylh ta skalúl7a, "nleq̓wlaq̓walúsem, xílemlhkan áti7, átsxen lhkúnsa ta ámha nskwt̓ús, meysantsútkan."

Cu7, nleq̓wlaq̓walúsem ku7 t̓elh láti7 ta skalúl7a. Nilh k̓a wi7 zaṁ ses ntsegtsgálus ta skalúl7a. Nleq̓wlaq̓walúsem ku7 aylh láti7, cu7, np̓ukwalúsnas ku7 aylh ki síkila, ki qwal̓ílha, tákem ku7 t̓u7 np̓ukwalúsnas.

Wa7 ku7 aylh láti7 ta skalúl7a, cw7aoz kwas katcúsma, nilh t̓u7 aylh sq̓áylecs ta sṁéṁlhatsa, q̓áylec. Cw7aoz k̓a wi7 put kw skekáẇs ku tmicws, wi7 sxwems kw stsicws úxwal̓.

Wa7 ku7 t̓u7 láti7, t̓iq ku7 t̓elh áti7 e ki slal̓íl̓teṁsa. *My*, tsa7cw ku7 aylh i slal̓íl̓teṁsa.

He took off with those things and he brought them to the Owl's place, where the Owl kept the girl. I guess that he knew the house of the Owl.

The girl was pondering what she would do, and she decided that she would run away. She made herself up, and she went to get tree-bark, all kinds of things. It's all kinds of things that the girl went for and prepared. She was going to fix her husband, and then she was going to run away from there.

The Owl had already set out hunting, looking for rabbits and everything that he used to bring: grouse, squirrels, he brought them to his *skiġw*, that is what he called her: *skiġw*. Whatever that is, I don't know what a *skiġw* is.

Nor did my grandmother tell me what a *skiġw* is. I guess that is what he made the girl into by keeping her as a wife.

So the girl was pondering what she would do, and she decided that she would run away. She said: "Oh, I'll go and look for tree-bark." She got tree-bark there, and pitch, everything.

Well, the Owl was on his way, and he arrived.

"Come then, Ápa7, come then." She was already made up, she was going to go home. "Open your eyes wide," she told the Owl, "open your eyes wide, this is what I have done, look how beautiful my face is, I have made myself up."

Oh, he opened his eyes wide, the Owl. That is why the Owl is still wide-eyed. He opened his eyes wide, and oh my, she poured into his eyes the tree-bark, the pitch, everything she poured into his eyes.

There he was, the Owl, he could not see, and the girl bolted and ran away, she ran away. Her land was not far away, I guess, so it did not take her long to get home.

So she arrived at her parents'. My, how glad her parents were.

Wa7 ku7 aylh káti7 ta sáẃta. Nilh ku7 t̓u7 stsut.s: "Huẏ t̓u7 t̓iq na skalúl7a, huż heṁ t̓u7 t̓íqmiṅas ts7a ta sṁéṁlhatsa." Tsut ku7 t̓elh i núkwa káti7: "Tay, nílhas láti7 ta sáẃta kwil̓ínal̓ap."

Cw7aoz ku7 t̓u7 kw sciṅs láti7, ts7as ku7 t̓elh ta skalúl7a, plan aylh wa7 nxwetsxwetsálus lhwas k̓a t̓u7 kenskelhnás i síkila múta7 i qwal̓ílha l ta nkwt̓ústeṅsa i takmá t̓u7 np̓ukwalúsnas ta skalúl7a. Cw7aoz ku7 t̓u7 kw sciṅs, t̓iq ku7 t̓elh ta skalúl7a. "Huhú hu, ts7ásmiṅlhkan na nskíġwa," tsut ku7, "huhú hu, ts7ásmiṅlhkan na nskíġwa."

Cu7, tsut ku7 t̓elh káti7 i tewtwúẃeta káti7 i wa7 estsetsítcw káti7 s7ístkna: "Náscit áku7, saẃt ti7 ta sṁéṁlhatsa, náscit áku7."

Cu7, tsut ku7 t̓elh ta skalúl7a: "Huhú hu, uts ti7 lhnílhas na nskíġwa, huhú hu, uts ti7 lhnílhas na nskíġwa," tsut ku7 t̓elh múta7 ta skalúl7a.

"Yekyíkalmicw i sreprápa," nilh ku7 t̓u7 szekzíkt.s i srápa.

Tsut ku7 t̓elh múta7: "Yekyíkalmicw i p̓eq̓wp̓áq̓ulha," nilh ku7 t̓u7 szekzíkt.s i p̓áq̓ulha káti7.

Tsut ku7 t̓elh: "Yekyíkalmicw i s7es7ístkna," nilh ku7 t̓u7 aylh szet̓q̓s i s7es7ístkna.

Nilh ku7 t̓u7 stsut.s ta pápel7a: "Hal̓acíti malh ta sáẃta ta skíġwsa, hal̓acíti." —plan wa7 súcwtnas kwas uts lhwas skiġws láti7 ta wa7 hal̓acítitas—"hal̓acíti."

Cu7, tsut ku7 káti7 i tewtwíẃta: "Huż q̓elza7stúm ta stsutálhkalha." Cu7, qwatsáts ku7 t̓elh p̓ámsem i sqáyqeycwa láti7 nq̓élza7tna, huż q̓elza7stwítas ta stsutálhiha. Plan láti7 wa7 ptínusem i tewtwúẃeta ta shúẏsa k̓ezaka7mínitas láti7 ta stsutálhiha.

But there was a slave there, who said: "He will come, the Owl, he will come for this girl." Then some other people said: "Hey, get that slave ready for the Owl."

It did not take long before the Owl came, he had already scratches on his eyes, because he'd been trying to take off the tree-bark and the pitch from his face, everything that she had poured into the Owl's eyes. It did not take long before the Owl arrived. "Hoohoo hoo, I have come for my *skiġw*," he said, "hoohoo hoo, I have come for my *skiġw*."

Oh my, the boys who were living in that underground house said: "Bring him that slave girl, bring her to him."

But the Owl said: "Hoohoo hoo, that is not my *skiġw*, hoohoo hoo, that is not my *skiġw*," he said again.

"Let the trees fall to the ground," and the trees fell down.

Next, he said: "May the storage caches fall to the ground," and the caches fell down.

Finally, he said: "May the underground houses fall in," and the underground houses collapsed.

Then someone said: "Show the poor guy his *skiġw*, show her to him"—he had already recognized that the one they had shown to him before was not his *skiġw*—"show her to him."

Then the boys said: "We are going to give our in-law a sweatbath." They went and made a fire in the sweatlodge where they were going to give their in-law a sweatbath. But the boys were in fact planning to kill their in-law.

Plan tsukw kw spámsmi. "Cuy," tsúnitas ku7 aylh ta stsutálhiha, "húy̓lhkacw nas q̓élza7, kwánlhkacw kelh ta skíġwswa." Cu7, qwatsatsstwítas ku7 ṫelh áku7 ta stsutálhiha, tsicwstwítas áku7, nq̓élza7tna láku7, cikiṅítas ku7 aylh áku7 nq̓élza7tna, tsiqiṅítas ku7 aylh, tseqtsiqiṅítas ku7 tu7, nilh ku7 ṫu7 tu7 aylh szuqws ta stsutálha.

Áti7 lhtseṁpás ta nsptákwlha. Cw7aoz heṁ ti7 kwas wenácw, sptakwlh ti7.

They had made the fire ready. "Come on," they told their in-law, "we are going to have a sweatbath, and then you will get your *skiġw*." Oh, they took off with their in-law, and they brought him to the sweatlodge, they pushed him into the sweatlodge, they stabbed him, they stabbed him all over, and then he died.

That is where my *sptakwlh* ends. It is not true, it is a *sptakwlh*.

7.

Ta sqáycwa uʼḷusmíntali ta míxalha

The Man Who Stayed with the Bear

TOLD BY BILL EDWARDS

(7) Ta sqáycwa ulʹlusmíntali ta míxalha

Icíṅas, wa7 ku7 ta pápel7a sqaycw, ta sem7ámsa, nkekalhás i stsmáĺt.sa, lkw7úna Nxwístna. Papt ku7 wa7 í7wa7 lhwas píxeṁ i ƙsáytkensa, cw7aoz ṫu7 kwas átṡxem ku staṁ, cw7aoz kwas zúqwnucw. Zúqwnucw ku7 i sneƙwnúƙwa7sa, kelhklhaẇsnítas i szuqwnucwíha, nmimeĺnítas, cw7aoz kwas úṁnem.

Pála7 ku7 aylh sgap láti7 wa7 sƙaĺemmínem ƙa e ki stsmáĺt.sa, nilh shuẏs ílalwit i stsmáĺt.sa, táytwit. Nilh ṫu7 stsúntanemwit e ta skicez7íha: "Tsukw malh s7ílallap! Lhṫíqas ta sqatsza7lápa, cw7it kelh ku s7ílhenlap."

Put ƙa ṫu7 ṫíqalmen ti7 ta sqáycwa, nilh sqaṅíms. Nilh ṫu7 sxaṫs ta scwákwekwsa, qwenúxwalhtṡa7, nilh ṫu7 sṗelƙúsems láti7, nilh sqwatsátss xáṫem e ta sqwéma.

Ṫak, xáṫem, tsicw npegpgánk ti7 áta7 sqáyt.sa ti7 ta sqwéma. Wa7 láti7 ta tsaĺálha. Nilh sláti7s lhgúẏtas.

Guẏt láti7 ṫu psiĺ, nilh sqwatsátss matq múta7, nilh ṫu7 ses káti7 matqsút. Wa7 ku7 tsut: "Húẏlhkan ṫu7 matq ṫu7 ṫu zúqwkan, cw7aoz kw nshuẓ úxwaĺ, húẏlhkan ṫu7 máṁteq ṫu7 kents7áwna ṫu7, zuqwcenlhkán kelh ṫu zúqwkan."

Ṫak ku7 káti7, nilh s7átṡxnas ta q̇wexq̇wíxqwa míxalh wa7 smítsa7q káti7 nklústsa. Nilh ṫu7 stṡiteṁmínas, cw7aoz káti7 kwas kensqúscitas. Wa7 séna7 cw7it i qwesmáĺtssa, ṫu7 cw7aoz káti7 kw squscitas.

Nilh ṫu7 sqwaĺút.stuṁ e ta míxalha: "Tay, nsnúƙwa7, áma ta nscwákwkwa ta scw7áysa kwásu qúscits. Wá7lhkan zewáten ta wa7 szaytenstúmihas i ƙsáytkenswa: cw7áysa ṫú7a kwásu zúqwnucw, cw7aoz kwas uṁentsíhaswit lhwas zúqwnucwwit. Lh7i7wa7míntsacw, lhszaytenmínacw stáṁas ku stsúntsin, húẏlhkan tsunáṁentsin kwa píxeṁ."

(7) The Man Who Stayed with the Bear

A long time ago there was a man who lived at Nxwísten with his wife and his three children. Whenever his friends would go out hunting he would go with them, but he never saw any game, and he never killed anything. When his friends had killed any game they would divide what they had killed and share it among themselves, but they would not give him anything.

One evening his children were waiting for him and they started to cry, because they were hungry. So their mother told them: "Stop your crying! When your father comes, you will have lots of food."

The man was already almost there, so he heard them. He took it really hard, and he got sad, so he turned around right there, and he left to go up the mountain.

He climbed his way up, and he got to the top of that mountain, where it is burned all over. There is a lake there. So that is where he slept.

He slept there till daybreak, and then he set out walking again, he just kept wandering around aimlessly. He said: "I am going to walk till I die, I am not going home, I am going to walk around this place, I will go without food till I die."

So he carried on, and then he saw a black bear sitting in front of him. He went up to him, but he did not want to shoot him. Although he had a lot of arrows, he did not shoot him.

Then the bear said to him: "Say, my friend, I am glad that you did not shoot me. I know what your friends have been doing to you: Because you never manage to kill any game, they don't give you from what you have killed. If you come with me, and if you do everything I tell you, I will teach you how to hunt."

Plan ku7 wa7 lhwáltsten láti7, nilh stsúnem e ta míxalha: "Húẏlhkacw i7wa7mínts, húẏlhkacw úllusmints tákem sútik." Ti7 ta míxalha, xzum ku7 ti7 ku sḱwaltss láti7 lt.sa wa7. Pála7 lt7úna sqút.sa ta sḱwáltsa láti7 ku7 lhwas wats, lt7u múta7 ta sqúta láti7 lhwas kósao7, lt7u múta7 ta sqúta wa7 ku7 láti7 ntaḱw ta qú7a, qúqu7, láti7 lhwas tiq úqwa7. "Lts7a lhwan wa7 tu qapts, wá7lhkan xátmintsin kw s7ullusmíntsacw."

Nilh ku7 tu7 stcúsems káti7 ta sqáycwa, cw7aoz kw s7átsxnas káti7 ku stam, ku s7ílhen. "Stámas malh kelh ku s7ílhenlhkalh?," wa7 ku7 ntsutánwas. Láti7 tu7, nilh tu7 szewátnas ta míxalha lhstámas ta wa7 sptínusems, nilh ku7 tu7 stsúnem: "Cw7aoz kwásu ptínusmin ku s7ílhen, wá7lhkan kelh úmentsin ku s7ílhen."

Nilh tu7 skákemcals ku7 aylh ki qwáltsa káti7, ḱúlem ta ngúẏttna. Xílem ku7 ta sqáycwa, qixtsánitas ti7 ta sḱwáltsa. "Lt7u kelh squta, láta7 kelh lhwacw guẏt, lts7a kelh s7éntsa," tsut ku7.

"Kélhen malh i stemtétemswa." Nilh ku7 tu7 aylh slhuquntsút.s ta sqáycwa, kelhnás ta téxw7atssa, kítsinas lt7úna; nilh skítslecs.

Neqwálts ku7, cw7aoz káti7 kwa sḱéḱxem nukwlh láti7 kwas ulhcw. Nilh múta7 ta súpsa ta míxalha wa7 kanukwa7stáliha kwas wa7 neqwálts. "Cwakantsílhkan kelh lhtsícwas kw shúẏlhkalh ílhen," tsut ku7 ta míxalha.

Tsemp ku7 áti7 ta tánamtna, cwakaném ku7. Nilh tu7 scwítscitem ta quta skwakst tixalaká7em káti7 ta míxalha. Nilh tu7 stsúnas: "Lkw7áwna cuy tṡumún ts7a ta nskwáksta." Nilh tu7 stṡumúnas ta skwákst.sa ta míxalha, ta qwetáka7sa aylh múta7 ta míxalha, nilh ti7 wa7 tṡumúnas snilh. Nilh ti7 ta wa7 száytni xw7útsin tánamten.

Qapts ku7 aylh, ligwtsánas ta sḱwáltsa ti7 ta míxalha, cwitscitém ku7 ta téxw7atssa, nilh tu7 szuhumtsínemnem.

It was already autumn, so the bear said to him: "You will come with me, you will stay with me all winter." That bear had a big cave where he stayed. On one side of the cave he would defecate, on another he would urinate, and on another side again there was water seeping through, a little well, and that is where he went to drink. "This is where I stay till spring, and I want you to keep me company."

The man looked around, but he didn't see any food. "I wonder what we are going to have for food," he thought. Right away the bear knew what he was thinking, so he told him: "Don't worry about food, I will give you food."

Then he gathered a bunch of fir branches and he made a bed. The man did the same and then they closed the cave. "You will sleep on that side, and I on this side," said the bear.

"Take off your clothes." The man undressed himself, he took off his bow and put it down; then he laid down himself.

It was warm in there, there wasn't even a bit of a draft coming in. It was the breath of the bear that was making it warm in the cave. "I will wake you up when it is time for us to eat," said the bear.

One month went by, and then the bear woke the man up. He held up one paw for him and he told him: "Come on, lick my paw right here." So he licked the bear's paw, and also the other paw, that is what he licked. They did that for four months.

Spring came around, and the bear opened the cave, he handed the man his bow, and he gave him farewell instructions.

Kwancitém ku7 ki xw7utsinálqwa, ki qwesmáĺtssa, nilh t̓u7 smaysnás iż. "Kwan izáwna," tsúnem ku7, "Lhqúscitacw ku stam̓, cw7aoz iż kwas cik̓. Cw7áozas kwásu qúsem ku q̓wexq̓wíxqw míxalh. Cw7aoz ku scwená7em kwas kacwena7mantsihása kw scw7ays kwásu zúqwnucw. Paptkácw kelh t̓u7 wa7 zúqwnucw lhwacw píxem̓. Cw7aoz kwas huż tayt i k̓sáytkenswa, i stsmáĺt.swa. Ku kéla7 szúqwnucwsu, cw7áozas̱ kw s7úm̓nacw ku swat, tsukw t̓u7 i k̓sáytkenswa, ta sem7ámswa múta7 i stsmáĺt.swa." Nilh ku7 t̓u7 aylh sqwáĺnem ká7as kelh lhwas púnas i tśí7a.

Nilh sqwatsátss ti7 ta sqáycwa, t̓ak ku7 t̓u7, tsicw e ta sxekcítma e ta míxalha, qúscitas ta xzúma sxwelácken. Nilh skwánas, nilh sk̓ihkmíńas aylh, nilh s7úxwaĺsas. T̓ak kent7ú ku scá7sa l ta swá7sa iż i núkwa úcwalmicw, káti7 ku7 lht̓ákas. Tsicw áti7 ta sem7ámsa, lt.sa wa7. Plan wa7 xaxeĺqwám̓ ku7 ta sem7ámsa, tsut kw splans wa7 szá7ten. Tákem sútik kw scw7ays kw swa7s ta kwtámtssa, nilh stsut.s kw splans tu7 wa7 zuqw.

Nilh t̓u7 stśaqwańítas ti7 ta tśí7a st̓íqcals, t̓iq átsxnem e ki núkwa úcwalmicw, cw7aoz kw s7um̓nás iż ku stam̓. Nilh ku7 t̓u7 sqlíli, tsútwit ku7: "Tsilkst t̓ánam̓ten kw scw7ays kwas t̓iq, pepla7úl tśi7 ta st̓íqcalsa. Plan t̓u7 wa7 áma kw spal7atsmíńas t̓u7 ti7, tśaqwańás t̓u7 snilh."

Qwatsáts ku7 múta7 píxem̓, úĺ̓usnas i tśí7a l ta pal7úlm̓ecwa láti7, nilh szúqwsas tákem. xw7útsin kw sq̓éq̓em̓ps tśi7 i zúqwsasa. Kwikws ku7 t̓u7 lhláti7 ta skwámsa, nilh iż úxwaĺsas. "U, qwenqwánt ta sqáycwa," tsúnem ku7 e ki núkwa úcwalmicw, "zúqwnucw k̓a núkuńa, kwikws ta st̓íqcalsa." Qwatsátswit ku7 aylh píxem̓ wi snilh, t̓ák.wit, cw7ay t̓u7 kw szúqwnucwi, tsukw t̓u7 ta st̓aláliha.

Wa7 ku7 ta pápel7a qelhmémeń l wi snilh, nilh ku7 t̓u7 stsut.s: "Zewatet.sás ti7 kwa píxem̓, wa7 t̓u7 zewátnas nká7as lhwas wa7 i tśí7a. Lh7ámhas kw sqwaĺút.saĺap, sxek um̓entumulhás kelh."

He took four of the man's arrows, and he fixed them.

"Take these," he told the man, "When you shoot anything with them, they won't miss. But don't shoot at any black bear. No Indian doctor will ever be able to put a spell on you so that you won't kill game. You will always kill some game when you go out hunting. Your relatives and your children will never be hungry. The first thing you kill, do not give it to anybody else but your kinsmen, your wife and your children." Then he told the man where he could find deer.

So the man took off, he walked on, and he got to the place the bear had told him about, where he shot a big buck. So he took it, he put it on his back, and he brought it home. He went up to the place where the other people lived, and he reached the place where his wife lived. His wife had already cut her hair, because she thought she had been widowed. All winter her husband had been away, so she thought that he had died already.

Well, they ate the venison that he had brought, and the other people came to see him, but he did not give them anything. So they got angry and said: "Five months he stays away, and then he brings only one deer. It's okay already that he eats it all by himself, let him eat it."

So he went out hunting again, he gathered the deer in one spot and he killed them all. Forty deer is what he killed. He took only a little bit, however, and that is what he brought home. "Oh, that poor guy," the other people said, "he killed some game again, but he brought only a little bit." Then they went out hunting themselves, but they did not kill anything, they only got tired.

There was one old man among them, and he said: "That man knows how to hunt, he knows where the deer are. If you talk to him nicely, he might give us some."

Tsicw ku7 aylh qwaĺut.stwítas láti7, nilh tu7 stsúnas i ucwalmícwa kw snási zacnálhtŝa7. Nq̓sańkminitás ku7, ntsutanwaswít tu7 kw spepla7úls tu7 ku szúqwnucws, nilh tu7 ses nq̓sańkmínitas. "Put ha kelh tákemlhkalh nas szacenstáli ku pépla7 tu7 tŝi7?"

Wa7 tu7 aylh tu7 qwatsátswit tu7 aylh tákem. *Gee* ku7 aylh, itsícwwitas, sxaw ti7 tu7, atŝxnítas, slhvk tu7 i tŝí7a. Suq̓wemwít ku7 aylh láti7, pála7 sq̓it, put, gap, psiĺ múta7 ta núkwa sq̓it. Put tu7 múta7 gap, ta núkwa sq̓it láti7 lhq̓wemtstwítas i tŝí7a.

Nilh stexws tu7 aylh xweystúm e ki nḱsáytkensa. Gélgel ku sqaycw, á7xa7 kwa píxem̓.

The people went and talked to him, and he told them to go and pack the meat. They laughed at him, because they thought he had killed only one deer, so they laughed at him. "Do we really all have to go to pack one deer?"

However, they all took off. Gee, when they got there, were they ever amazed, they saw deer plopped down everywhere. They were busy skinning the whole day and evening, and the next day from daybreak on. It got evening again, and the day after that they brought all the deer home.

From that time on the man was really loved by his people. He had become a strong man, good at hunting.

Lillooet-English Glossary

Grammatical terms:

adh.	adhortative particle (enclitic)
adv.	adverb
art.	article
aux.	auxiliary proclitic phrase
compl.	completive particle (enclitic)
concl.	conclusive particle (enclitic)
conf.	confirming particle (enclitic)
conj.	conjunction
dem.	demonstrative pronoun
dem./adv.	demonstrative adverb
disc.	general discourse particle (enclitic)
emph.	emphatic particle (enclitic)
excl.	exclamation
expr.	expression
hyp.	hypothesizing particle (enclitic)
infl.	inflected form
int.	interrogative
interj.	interjection
irr.	irrealis particle (enclitic)
kat.	kataphoric pronoun
n.	noun
num.	numeral
pers.	personal pronoun
pot.	potential particle (enclitic)
prep.	preposition
pres.	presuppositional particle (enclitic)
qu.	question particle (enclitic)
rep.	reportative particle (enclitic)
res.	resultative
sent./equ.	sentence equivalent
v./intr.	intransitive verb
v./tr.	transitive verb

Other abbreviations:

esp.	especially
F	Fountain (northern) dialect
M	Mount Currie (southern) dialect
s.o.	someone
s.t.	something

For further information on the organization of this glossary, and for general information on the grammatical structure of Lillooet, including the various categories indicated by the above abbreviations, please see the Introduction to his volume. More detailed information (e.g., on categories like "sentence equivalents," or "pivoting/non-pivoting" in the demonstrative adverbial system) is available in Van Eijk (1997).

álas   *v./intr.* very, really
álk̓wen   *v./tr.* to babysit s.o.
álk̓wilh   *v./intr.* to babysit
áma   *v./intr.* good
áma ta nscwákwkwa   *expr.* I am glad (*áma* "good;" *scwákwekw* "heart")
ananáh   *excl.* ouch!
ápa7   *n.* (term of endearment to address a man or boy, roughly translatable as "mate," "buddy" or "good friend")
an̓waszánucw   *num.* two years old
áti7   *dem./adv.* that way (visible, non-pivoting)
átsxcit   *v./tr.* to see s.t. that belongs to s.o.
átsxem   *v./intr.* to (be able to) see, have vision
átsxen   *v./tr.* to see s.o., s.t. (*átsxnem* "he is/was seen")
aylh   *adv.* and then, next
á7en̓was   *num.* two animals (*án̓was* "two")
á7han   *excl.* see?, didn't I tell you?
á7hantsu   *excl.* see?, didn't I tell you?
á7xa7   *v./intr.* talented, blessed, very good at s.t.
cátlec   *v./intr.* to get out of s.t.
cá7sa   (short for *lti scá7sa*) *infl.* upwards from (*ca7* "high")
celhantsút   *v./intr.* to offer one's help, to volunteer
cíkin̓   *v./tr.* to push s.o.
cik̓   *v./intr.* to miss a target
cin̓   *v./intr.* long (time)
cucwżálhcw   *n.* ant-hill
cuy   *excl.* o.k., come on, let's (do it)
cuy malh zam̓   *expr.* o.k., well then
cuy qa7 zam̓   *expr.* alright, o.k.
cu7   *excl.* oh boy!, my!

cwak *v./intr.* to wake up
cwákan̓ *v./tr.* to wake s.o. up
cwena7mán *v./tr.* to put a spell on s.o.
cwik̓áz̓ *n.* prepared salmon
cwíl̓em *v./intr.* to look for s.o., s.t.
cwilh *concl.* after all, as it turned out to be
cwítścit *v./tr.* to hand s.t. over to s.o.
cw7ay t̓u7 *expr.* not (at all) (*cw7aoz* "not, no;" with regular change to *cw7ay* before *t̓u7*)
cw7aoz *sent./equ.* not, no
cw7aoz káti7 *expr.* not at all
cw7aoz nukwlh *expr.* not at all
cw7áozas *infl.* (1) let it not be so; (2) (short for *lhcw7áozas*) if not
cw7it *v./intr.* much, many
e *prep.* (1) towards, (2) by (in passive constructions)
em7ímnem *v./intr.* to make animal noise (hoot, chirp, etc.)
estsetsítcw *v./intr.* to have houses (*tsitcw* "house")
estsítcw *v./intr.* to have a house
estsmál̓t *v./intr.* to have children
estsúwa7 *v./intr.* to own
et7úna *dem./adv.* that way, right along there (visible, pivoting)
ets7á *dem./adv.* this way, like this
gápalmen *v./intr.* to become evening
gélgel *v./intr.* strong
gelílc *v./intr.* to try hard, to do one's best
guẏt *v./intr.* to sleep
gwelín *n.* stomach
ha *qu.* question marker
hál̓acit *v./tr.* to show s.t. to s.o.
hem̓ *conf.* (generally indicates information that confirms the speaker's intention or his/her assessment of a situation, as in *wá7lhkan hem̓ kelh t̓u7 lts7a, wa7 malh wá7wi!* "I am just going to stay here, but you folks go right ahead!")
húhu7 *v./intr.* more, longer
huẏ *v./intr.* to be about to do s.t. (variant of *huz̓*, as in *huẏ t̓u7* "she/he is about to do smt.")

húýlhkacw *infl.* you will (are about to) do it (*huż* "to be about to do s.t.;" with regular change *ż* > *ý* before *-lhkacw* "you")
i *art.* (plural, present, known)
icíṅas *infl.* a long time ago (*ciṅ* "to last a long time")
ílal *v./intr.* to cry
ílalmin *v./tr.* to cry for s.o., s.t.
iż *dem.* those (there, visible)
í7wa7 *v./intr.* to accompany, come along
í7wa7min *v./tr.* to go with s.o.
ka *irr.* would, should
ka..a *res.* suddenly, not having full control, managing to do s.t.
kacíṁa *v./intr.* to disappear (temporarily) (*-ciṁ-* "to disappear")
kagúýta *v./intr.* to fall asleep (*guýt* "to sleep")
kákeṁcal *v./intr.* to collect, pick things up
káku7 *dem./adv.* around there (not visible, non-pivoting)
kálim *v./intr.* to follow
kalhaszánucw *num.* three years old
kalhéxwa *v./intr.* to appear suddenly (*-lhexw-* "to appear suddenly")
kalhmv́ka *v./intr.* to come off rotting (*lhvmk* "broken, not usable anymore")
kamulmulmúla *v./intr.* to stay dipped in all the time (*-mul-* "dipped in")
kánem *v./intr.* (*int.*) to do what, why, how?
kanmás ḱa *infl.* one way or the other (*kánem* "to do what, why, how?")
kanuḱwa7státiha *infl.* the one that is able to help
kasts *v./tr.* (*int.*) to do s.t. how to s.t.?
káta7 *dem./adv.* along there, around there (visible, non-pivoting)
katcúsma *v./intr.* to be able to see (*tcúsem* "to look around")
katékwa *v./intr.* to hush
katéqsa *v./tr.* to be able to catch s.t. (*kateqskaná kelh* "I will be able to catch it")
káti7 *dem./adv.* around here/there (visible, non-pivoting)
kat́éḱa *v./intr.* to hush, fall silent

katíla *v./intr.* to wait, stay put
katsésa *v./intr.* to get stretched (*-tses-* "to stretch")
katsáqwsa *v./tr.* to be able to eat s.t. (*cw7aoz kw skatsáqwsasa* "she could not eat it")
kaxílha *infl.* to work out, succeed (*-xilh-* "to be done in a certain way")
ka7átsxma *v./intr.* to be able to see (*átsxem* "to see")
ka7lh *adv.* for a while
kekáẃ *v./intr.* far away
kék7aẃ *v./intr.* a little bit farther (*ká7eẃ* "farther;" *-kaw-* "far")
kéla7 *v./intr.* (1) first; (2) very (as in *kéla7 q̓ix* "very hard")
kela7úl *v./intr.* the very first
kelh *pot.* (indicates that s.t. may happen or is likely to happen)
kélhen *v./tr.* to take s.t. off
kelhklháẃsen *v./tr.* to divide s.t. totally (*klháẃsen* "to divide s.t.')
kelhpáka7min *v./tr.* to let s.t. slip through one's hands
kém̓em *v./intr.* to dig edible roots
ken *prep.* around
kenskelhnás *infl.* he tried to take it off (*kélhen* "to take s.t. off")
kensqúscit *v./tr.* to want to shoot s.o. (*qúscit* "to shoot s.o.")
kent7ú *dem./adv.* around there (visible, pivoting)
ki *art.* (plural, present, known; variant of the article *i* which changes to *ki* after *e* "towards," "by," *l* "in, on, at, *lhel* "from," and *ken* "around")
kíka7 *n.* (term of endearment to address a woman or girl, roughly translatable as "dear" or "darling")
kítsiṅ *v./tr.* to put s.t. down
kítslec *v./intr.* to lay oneself down
kí7keɬ *v./intr.* lazy, unwilling to do s.t.
klháka7cit *v./tr.* to release, let go of s.t. that then hits s.o. else
kósao7 *v./intr.* to urinate (used only for men and animals)
ksnan *v./tr.* to send s.o. on an errand
ku *art.* (singular, present or absent, unknown)
ku *dem./adv.* (short form of *ekw7ú* "that way," in *ku scá7sa*

l ta swá7sa iż i núkwa úcwalmicw "That way to the high spot where the other people lived")
kúkuṅ   *v./tr.* to cook s.t.
kúkwcit   *v./tr.* to cook (*kukw*) s.t. for (*-cit*) s.o.
ku7   *rep.* as I was told
k̓a   *hyp.* I guess, it seems
k̓a malh   *conj.* but
k̓aláṅmiṅ   *v./tr.* to listen to s.o.
k̓áḷem   *v./intr.* to wait
k̓áḷemmin   *v./tr.* to wait for s.o.
k̓ezáka7min   *v./tr.* to murder s.o.
k̓ihkmíṅ   *v./tr.* to put s.t. on one's back
k̓sáytken   *n.* friend, relative, kinsman
k̓úḷem   *v./intr.* to make things
k̓úḷtsaṅ   *v./tr.* to make food, get food for s.o.
kw   *art.* (used with proper names and *swéta7* "so-and-so")
kw   *conj.* that
kwa   (short for *ku wa7* "the one that is not there yet")
kwam   *v./intr.* to take, get s.t.
kwan   *v./tr.* to take, get s.t.
kwáncit   *v./tr.* to take s.t. for s.o. (*húylhkacw nas, kwáncits ku cwik̓áż* "you will go and get me some prepared salmon"), to (temporarily) take s.t. away from s.o. (*kwancitém ku7 ki xw7utsinálqwa* "he took four arrows (from the man)")
kwelh   *art.* (plural, present or absent, unknown)
kwenswá   *aux.* that I am
kwikws   *v./intr.* little, a little bit
kwikws7úl   *v./intr.* too small
kwiḷín   *v./tr.* to get s.o., s.t. ready
kwíḷqscit   *v./tr.* to aim at s.o., s.t.
kwtamts   *n.* husband
kwt̓ústsa   (short for *eti skwt̓ústsa*)   *infl.* up to his face (*skwt̓us* "face;" *-s* "his" > *-ts* after *s*)
l   *prep.* in, on, at
lan   (short for *plan*)   *v./intr.* already
lánsa   (short for *ta slánsa*)   *infl.* because already

láti7 tu7 *expr.* right away
lílq *v./intr.* easy
lts7a *dem./adv.* here (visible, pivoting)
lts7áwna *dem./adv.* right here (visible, pivoting)
lhápen *v./tr.* to forget s.t.
lhas *aux.* when it is
lhá7sa (short for *lti slhá7sa*) *infl.* close to s.t. (*lha7* "close")
lhel *prep.* from
lhelkw7ú *dem./adv.* from there (non-visible, pivoting)
lhelt7ú *dem./adv.* from there (visible, pivoting)
lhelts7á *dem./adv.* from here (visible, pivoting)
lhelts7áwna *dem./adv.* right from here (visible, pivoting)
lhkúnsa *adv.* now
lhlak *v./intr.* from the ones (who are/were there)
lhq́íq́at *v./intr.* short
lhtákas *infl.* that he went (*tak* "to go")
lhúmun *v./tr.* to put s.t. on
lhuq́uṅtsút *v./intr.* to undress oneself
lhwal *v./intr.* to be left behind
lhwálen *v./tr.* to leave s.o., s.t. behind
lhwáltsten *n.* fall (season), autumn
lhwas *aux.* that he is
malh *adh.* then (as in English "do it then!")
mámteq *v./intr.* to walk, go for a walk
matq *v./intr.* to walk, go on foot
matqsút *v./intr.* to wander around aimlessly
máyscit *v./tr.* to fix s.t. for s.o.
mekilólya7 *n.* kind of sticky oil
méqwens *v./tr.* to put s.t. in one's mouth
mes *v./intr.* but (almost always combined with *tu7*)
meysantsút *v./intr.* to make oneself up
mítsa7q *v./intr.* to sit down
míxalh *n.* black bear
múltsam *v./intr.* to dip one's mouth into s.t.
múta7 *adv.* and, again
m7ámmin *v./tr.* to keep s.o. as a wife
na *art.* (singular, absent, known) F
náhen *v./tr.* to call s.o. such-and-such, to give s.o. a name

nas *v./intr.* to go (also pronounced *ṅas*, which may be standard for some speakers, although all occurrences in the texts are standardized to *nas*, due to the fact that the difference between *nas* and *ṅas* is very difficult to hear)

náscit *v./tr.* to bring s.t. to s.o. (perhaps also *ṅáscit*, see *nas* for the initial *n* or *ṅ*)

naxwít *n.* snake

neqwál̓ts *v./intr.* warm in the house

ngúy̓tten *n.* bed

nilh *kat.* (refers ahead to s.o. or s.t., as in *nílhas ti skwékwza7sa tsetsewq̓íṅkst* "it turned out be his own cub;" *nílha cwilh k̓a i stsmal̓tkálha sq̓welcitúmulhas* "it is our children that she cooked for us")

nílha *kat.* (form of *nilh*)

nilh t̓u7 *sent./equ.* (and) then, (and) so

nílhas *infl.* it turned out to be so-and-so

ni7 *dem.* that (there, invisible)

nkekalhás *num.* three people (*kalhás* "three")

nklus *n.* front area (*nklústsa* "in front of him")

nk̓yap *n.* coyote (*ta nk̓yápa* "the/a coyote;" *nk̓yáplhkan* "I am a coyote")

nkwt̓ústeṅ *n.* eye

nlep̓cálten *n.* garden

nleq̓wlaq̓walúsem *v./intr.* to open one's eyes wide

nlíġwtsaṅ *v./tr.* to open s.t. (particularly an entrance)

nlhaṁán *v.tr.* to put s.t. into s.t.

nlháṁcal *v./intr.* to serve oneself, put food on one's plate or into one's bowl

nlháṁqaṅ *v./tr.* to put s.o., s.t. on the bottom of s.t.

nlhá7cten *n.* ladder

nmíml̓en *v./tr.* to share s.t.

npegpgánk *v./intr.* burned all over (area)

npíġwqaṁ *v./intr.* to open one's bum

np̓ukwalúsen *v./tr.* to pour s.t into s.o.'s eyes

nq̓élza7ten *n.* sweatlodge

nq̓sáṅkmin *v./tr.* to laugh at s.o.

nt̓ak̓w *v./intr.* to pour out, seep through

ntsegtsgálus *v./intr.* big-eyed (as if one's eyes are torn open)

ntsqústen *n.* pot
ntsáqwqaṅ *v./tr.* to eat s.o.'s bum (*ntsaqwqáṅem* "her bum was eaten")
ntśítemmin *v./tr.* to go up to s.o.
núkuṅ, núkuṅa *adv.* again (often indicating amusement or aggravation)
nukw *v./intr.* other, another (*na núkwa* "the/an other one," *i núkwa* "some of them")
nukwlh *adv.* at all F (used only in *cw7aoz nukwlh* "not at all")
nxwetsxwetsálus *v./intr.* to have scratches on one's eyes
Nxwísten *n.* Bridge River
pál7atsmiṅ *v./tr.* to eat s.t. by oneself
pal7úlṁecw *num.* one spot
pápla7 *num.* one person (*pála7* "one thing")
papt *v./intr.* always
pépla7 *num.* one animal (*pála7* "one thing;" *pepla7lhkácw* "you are another one," literally "you are one animal")
pepla7úl *num.* just one animal
píxem *v./intr.* to hunt
plan *v./intr.* already
plans *v./intr.* already, while something else happened
psil̂ *v./intr.* daylight
ptakwlh *v./intr.* to tell a legend
ptákwlhmin *v./tr.* to tell a legend about s.o. or s.t.
ptínusem *v./intr.* to think, plan
pun *v./tr.* to find s.o., s.t.
put *v./intr.* enough, just right
put t̂u7 *expr.* right away
pu7ẏacwám *v./intr.* to hunt mice (*pú7ẏacw* "mouse;" *-am* "to get, catch s.t.")
pzan *v./tr.* to meet s.o. (*pzánas* "he met him")
ṗámsem *v./intr.* to make a fire
ṗáq̇ulh *n.* cache, storage shed
ṗegṗíġlha *n.* frog
ṗelk̇úsem *v./intr.* to turn around
qaṁt.s *v./tr.* to hit s.o., s.t.
qaṅím *v./intr.* to hear

qańímens *v./tr.* to hear s.o., s.t. (*qańimenswítkacw* "you heard them")
qapts *n.* spring (season)
qa7 *pres.* as you should know, after all, in fact
qá7eżmin *v./tr.* to get tired of s.o., s.t.
qel̓qel̓tsíń *v./intr.* to beg
qemp *v./intr.* hot
qíqtśem *v./intr.* to chew
qíqtśmiń *v./tr.* to chew on s.t.
qlil *v./intr.* angry
qul *v./intr.* full
qu7 *n.* water
qvl *v./intr.* bad
q̓áylec *v./intr.* to jump, run away
q̓elcán7an *v./tr.* to jump over s.o., s.t.
q̓élza7 *v./intr.* to take a sweatbath
q̓élza7s *v./tr.* to give s.o. a sweatbath
q̓ix *v./intr.* hard, firm
q̓íxtsań *v./tr.* to close an opening
q̓mínen *v./tr.* to throw s.o. down
qwal̓ílh *n.* pitch (from tree)
qwal̓ts *n.* fir branch
qwal̓út.s *v./tr.* to speak to s.o.
qwatsáts *v./intr.* to set out, to leave
qwatsátss *v./tr.* to set out, leave with s.o.
qwáxtmin *v./tr.* to notice s.o., s.t. (*qwaxtminitás ku7* "they noticed him, as I was told")
qwenqwánt *v./intr.* poor
qwenúxwalhtśa7 *v./intr.* sad
qwesmál̓ts *n.* arrow
qwiqws *v./intr.* small
q̓wel *v./intr.* cooked
q̓wels *v./tr.* to cook s.t.
q̓weml̓s *v./tr.* to own it all, bring it all home
q̓wetáka7 *n.* one hand
q̓wexq̓wíxqw *v./intr.* black animal
saw̓t *n.* slave; pitiful person

scécem̓ *v./intr.* silly, irresponsible
scúcwez̓ *n.* ant
scwená7em *n.* Indian doctor
scw7ays *infl.* that it is not (*cw7aoz* not, no, with regular change *z > y* before *-s* and *ao > a* before *y*)
selts7ás *infl.* that it is there (*lts7a* "here (visible, pivoting);" *s-* "that it is;" *-s* "its")
séna7 *adv.* (indicates something that is denied or contradicted later, and translates more or less as "should be, supposed to be")
ses *aux.* that it is
sgap *n.* evening
síkil *n.* tree-bark
síma7 *v./intr.* come!
síma7min *v./tr.* come for it, come to get it!
sit.st *n.* night
skalúla7 *n.* (great horned) owl
skícza7 *n.* mother
skig̓w *n.* beloved person, sweetheart, darling (probably used only for women)
skits *infl.* lying down (*-kits-* "to lie down;" *s-* "ongoing state")
sk̓ék̓xem̓ *n.* breeze, draft
sk̓úk̓wm̓it *n.* child, young person
sk̓ul̓ *n.* what one makes
skwakst *n.* hand, paw
skwam *n.* what s.o. takes
skwékwza7 *n.* child, offspring
skwezkwékwza7 *n.* children, offspring
skwt̓us *n.* face
sk̓wal̓ts *n.* cave
sk̓wemk̓úk̓wm̓it *n.* children (*sk̓úk̓wm̓it* "child")
sk̓wilh *n.* left-over (food)
slhvk *v./intr.* plopped down
smítsa7q *v./intr.* to sit, be sitting
smul *v./intr.* dipped in (*-mul-* "to get dipped in;" *s-* "ongoing state")
smúlhats *n.* woman F (means "girl" in *wa7 ku7 aylh láti7 ptínusem ta smúlhatsa lhhúz̓as kánem* "the girl was pondering what she would do," in the story about the girl

and the Owl)
sṁémlhats *n.* girl F
sṁúṁteṁ *n.* grouse (bird)
snástsu *infl.* that you go (*nas* "to go;" *s*- "that it is;" -*tsu* "your")
snek̓wnúk̓wa7 *n.* friends (*snúk̓wa7* "friend")
snilh *pers.* he, she
snúk̓wa7 *n.* friend (*na snúk̓wa7sa* "his friend")
snúwa *pers.* you (singular)
sptakwlh *n.* legend
sptínusem *n.* thought
sqátsza7 *n.* father
sqaycw *n.* man
sqayt *n.* mountain top
sqiqtś *n.* what s.o. chews
sq̓it *n.* day, weather
sq̓ut *n.* side
sqwáłen *v./tr.* to report to s.o.
sqwem *v./intr.* piled up
sqweyíts *n.* rabbit
sq̓waxt *n.* foot
srap *n.* tree
stag̓észa *n.* squirrel
staṁ *int.* what? (*ku staṁ* "anything")
stáṁas k̓a *expr.* it must be something, whatever it is
stemtéteṁ *n.* clothing, clothes
steqs *v./tr.* to hold on to s.t.
stexw *v./intr.* reall(ly), very
stak *infl.* s.o.'s going (*ti stáksa* "his going")
stalhálam *n.* grizzly bear
stíqcal *n.* what s.o. brings
stsmalt *n.* children, offspring
stsetsew̓qíṅkst (also *tsetsew̓qíṅkst*) *n.* bear cub (literally: "the one with marks (*stsétsew̓*) on it's claws (-*qiṅkst*)")
stsicw *n.* what one goes to get
stsitsá7 *n.* crow
stutálh *n.* son-in-law, male in-law
stsut.s *infl.* he said something (literally "the fact of his saying;" *tsut* "to say something, to think;" *s*- "the fact of;"

-*s* "his, her, its")
su *aux.* that you are doing s.t.
súcwten *v./tr.* to recognize s.o.
supˈ *n.* breath
súq̓wem *v./intr.* to skin animals
sútik *n.* winter
súxwast *v./intr.* to go down
swat *int.* who?
swéta7 *pers.* so-and-so (*u, kw swéta7* "oh, that so-and-so," meaning "oh, that Grizzly!" in "Grizzly Bear and Black Bear's Children")
sxaw *n.* surprise
sxek *adv.* maybe
sxílem *n.* what happens to s.o., what s.o. does
sxwelácken *n.* buck (male deer)
száyten *n.* what s.o. does
száytenmin *v./tr.* to do s.t., carry out a task
száytens *v./tr.* to do s.t. to s.o.
szá7ten *n.* widow, widower
s7á7tseq *n.* bottom of a tree
s7éntsa *pers.* I, me
s7ílhen *n.* food F
s7ístken *n.* underground house
s7útsez *v./intr.* ready, all set
ta *art.* (singular, present, known) F
tákem *v./intr.* all
tákem swat *expr.* everybody
tay *excl.* say!, hey!
tayt *v./intr.* hungry F
tcúsem *v./intr.* to look up, around
téxw7ats *n.* bow (of bow and arrow)
tewtwúw̓et *n.* boys (*twúw̓et* "boy")
ti *art.* (singular, present, known) M
ti skicez7íha *infl.* their mother (*skícza7* "mother;" with regular change to *skicez7-* before *-i* "their," the latter with regular change to *-ih* before *a*)
ti slánsa *infl.* because already (*lan* "already")
ti sqatsez7íha *infl.* their father (*sqátsza7* "father;" with regular change to *sqatsez7-* before *-i* "their," the latter

with regular change to -*ih* before *a*)
ti7 *dem.* that (there, visible)
tmicw *n.* land
t.sa *aux.* that s.o. is
tu7 *compl.* (indicates that s.t. is over and done with)
twiẃt *n.* boy
ƛak *v./intr.* (1) to go along; (2) to get ..er (as in *ƛak qemp* "it got hotter")
ƛalál *v./intr.* tired
ƛámin *n.* fur, animal hair
ƛaq̓ *v./intr.* to cross, go across
ƛelh *adv.* after that
ƛépa *v./intr.* (short for *kaƛépa*) to get dark
ƛík̓lec *v./intr.* to stretch oneself
ƛiq *v./intr.* to arrive here
ƛíqalmen *v./intr.* to be about to get here
ƛíqcit *v./tr.* to bring s.t. to s.o.
ƛíqmiṅ *v./intr.* to arrive here for s.o., s.t.
ƛiqs *v./tr.* to bring s.o., s.t. here
ƛit *adv.* also
ƛixalaká7em *v./intr.* to hold up one's hands
ƛk̓íwlec *v./intr.* to climb a tree
ƛu *conj.* until
ƛu7 *disc.* well, but, so (*ƛú7a* has *a* echoing the final *a* of *lhá7sa* in *lhá7sa ƛú7a ti qú7a* "close to the water")
ƛu7 snilhts *conj.* and then
tsaƛálh *n.* lake
tsáma *v./intr.* to have a hard time, lose energy for s.t.
tsáẃtswa *n.* the poor thing
tsa7cw *v./intr.* glad
tseḿp *v./intr.* to end
tseqtsíqiṅ *v./tr.* to stab s.o. all over
tseq.wálaka7 *v./intr.* to open one's arms
tsetseẃqíṅkst (same as *stsetseẃqíṅkst*, see there)
tsicw *v./intr.* to get there
tsícwalmen *v./intr.* to get close to, to almost get there
tsilkst *num.* five
tsíqiṅ *v./tr.* to stab s.o.

tsitcw *n.* house
tsukw *v./intr.* only; finished, all done
tsun *v./tr.* to tell s.o. s.t. (*tsúnem* "he was told")
tsut *v./intr.* to say s.t., to think
tsúwa7 *pers.* s.o.'s own
ts7a *dem.* this (visible)
ts7as *v./intr.* to come
ts7ásmiṅ *v./tr.* to come for s.o., s.t.
ts7áwna *dem.* this one right here (visible)
tśáqwan *v./tr.* to eat s.t.
tśemqán *v./tr.* to pull s.t. apart
tśeqp *v./intr.* to get stuck (sticky matter)
tśeqpán *v./tr.* to stick s.t. on s.t.
tśíla *v./intr.* just like
tśíla nka7 *expr.* how? (*tśíla* "just like;" *nka7* "where?")
tśilawílc *v./intr.* the same size
tśi7 *n.* deer, meat, venison
tśla7 *n.* basket (*esp.*, berry-basket)
tśuṁún *v./tr.* to lick s.t.
tśúquṁ *n.* chickadee
úcwalmicw *n.* person, Indian
ucwalmícwtsmiṅ *v./tr.* to tell a story in Indian about s.o., s.t.
úllusen *v./tr.* to gather them, bring them together
úllusmin *v./tr.* to stay with s.o., to keep s.o. company
ulhcw *v./intr.* to enter
úlhcwmin *v./tr.* to get into s.t., to enter (*ulhcwmínem* "she was entered")
úṁen *v./tr.* to give s.t. to s.o. (as a gift, not just handing s.t. over)
úqwa7 *v./intr.* to drink
uts *sent./equ.* to be not the one
utszílc *v./intr.* to sit down firmly, to fix oneself
úxwal *v./intr.* to go home
úxwals *v./tr.* to take s.o., s.t. home
wats *v./intr.* to defecate F
wayt *v./intr.* to suffer, to have a hard time
wa7 *v./intr.* to be (busy with)
wa7s *v./tr.* to keep s.o. somewhere

wenácw *v./intr.* true
wéna7 *interj.* uhm (*kwánas i..wéna7..zútsmensa* "he took her..uhm..paint")
weqw *v./intr.* to get carried away by the water, to drown
wi *art.* (used with plural proper nouns or plural pet names, as in *wi stsetsewqínkst* "the bear cubs," or with personbal pronouns, as in *wi snilh* "they")
wínacw *v./intr.* alike
wi7 *emph.* (meaning elusive, probably indicates a certain emphasis, usually combined with *ka*)
wi7 *conj.* and so
xat ta scwákwekwsa *expr.* he was sad, took it hard (**xat** "difficult, having a hard time," *scwákwekw* "heart")
xátem *v./intr.* to go up, go uphill
xátmin *v./tr.* to like, want s.t.
xáwen *v./intr.* low, below
xawxawxáwna (short for *l ti xawxawxáwna*) *infl.* all along the low part (*xáwen* "low")
xáxelqwam *v./intr.* to cut one's hair (e.g., as a sign of mourning)
xekcít *v./tr.* to tell, explain s.t. to s.o.
xílem *v./intr.* to do s.t. this or that way, be just like s.o. or s.t. (*xílem áti7* "to do s.t. like this")
xílhtumc *infl.* (inflected form of *xilhts* "to do s.t. to s.o.")
xilhts *v./tr.* to do s.t. to s.o. or s.t. in a certain way (*wa7 xilhtsas ets7á* "he was doing that;" *kánem su xílhtumc ets7á* "why did you do this to me?;" with regular dropping of *-ts* before *-tumc* "me")
xí7xew *v./intr.* raw, uncooked
xlíten *v./tr.* to invite s.o., call for s.o.
xzum *v./intr.* big
x7ilh *n.* other side
xwem *v./intr.* fast
xwem tu7 *expr.* sure enough
xweys *v./tr.* to like, love s.o.
xw7útsin *num.* four (*xw7útsin kw sqéqemps* "forty animals")
xw7utsinálqw *num.* four arrows (or any stick-like objecs)
yekyíkalmicw *v./intr.* to fall down to the ground (many

things)
zacnálhtśa7   *v./intr.* to pack meat, game
zact   *v./intr.* long
zaṁ   *adv.* after all, as things are now, as things turned out to be
zeƚq̓   *v./intr.* to fall in, topple over
zewáten   *v./tr.* to know s.o., s.t. (*zewatentsálitas* "they know me;" *ta wa7 zewátnan* "what I know")
zewatet.s   *v./tr.* to have learned s.t., to have acquired a skill
zuhumtsínmen   *v./tr.* to bid farewell to s.o., give s.o. final instructions
zuqw   *v./intr.* to die
zúqwcen   *v./intr.* to starve
zúqwnucw   *v./intr.* to kill game
zuqws   *v./tr.* to kill s.o. (*i zúqwsasa* "the ones he killed")
zútśmen   *n.* paint

Other books in the
First Nations Language Readers series:

wawiyatācimowinisa /
ᐊᐧᐃᔭᐨᒥᐃᓂᐢ /
Funny Little Stories
narrated by Cree-speaking students,
instructors, and Elders;
edited by Arok Wolvengrey

Nēnapohš āhtahsōkēwinan/
ᓀᓇᐳᕁ ᐊᐦᑕᐦᓲᑫᐃᐧᓇᐣ/
Nēnapohš Legends
narrated by Saulteaux Elders;
transcribed, translated and edited
by Margaret Cote

Ákaitsinikssiistsi /
Blackfoot Stories of Old
written, translated, and edited by
Ikkináínihki Lena Heavy Shields Russell
and Piitáákii *Inge Genee*

nīhithaw ācimowina /
ᓈᐦᐃᖬᐤ ᐊᒋᒧᐃᐧᓇ /
Woods Cree Stories
Written and translated by
Solomon Ratt